D1500613

Home From the Field

HOME *From the* FIELD

Collected Poems

Leo Dangel

Spoon River Poetry Press 1997

Home From the Field
published by
Spoon River Poetry Press
David Pichaske, editor
Post Office Box 6
Granite Falls, Minnesota 56241

Publication of this book is supported in part with funds provided by the Gunlogson Regional Research Fund and the Southwest State University Rural/Regional Studies Program.

ISBN 0-944024-31-9

In memory of my mother and father,
Sylvia and John Dangel

CONTENTS

Old Man Brunner Country (1987)

The Stones Take the Field

Old Man Brunner Country

PART I ❋ THE HAND ON THE SHOULDER

PASSING THE ORANGE

On Halloween night
the new teacher gave a party
for the parents.
She lined up the women
on one side of the schoolroom,
the men on the other,
and they had a race,
passing an orange
under their chins along each line.
The women giggled like girls
and dropped their orange
before it got halfway,
but it was the men's line
that we watched.
Who would have thought
that anyone could get them
to do such a thing?
Farmers in flannel shirts,
in blue overalls and striped overalls.
Stout men embracing one another.
Our fathers passing the orange,
passing the embrace—the kiss
of peace—complaining
about each other's whiskers,
becoming a team, winning the race.

GATHERING STRENGTH

I looked over my shoulder
at the bedroom mirror and flexed my biceps.
I inspected my body and studied
the body of Charles Atlas in a comic book.

One time, Old Man Brunner winked
and told me how to build muscles—
every day carry a calf for ten minutes
until it's a cow and you're a gorilla.

In the barn, I bent over the calf,
put my left arm under the neck,
my right arm behind the back legs,
and stood up, the calf across my chest.

I marched in giant steps around the pen.
I dreamed about the people who would come
from all over to watch. The headlines
would say: Boy Carries Full-Grown Steer.

But through the dusty window, I looked
hard at the steers in the feedlot,
their blocky shoulders bumping for space
at the feedbunk. I set the calf down.

PA

When we got home, there was our old man
hanging by his hands from the windmill vane,
forty feet off the ground, his pants down,
inside out, caught on his shoes—he never wore
underwear in summer—shirt tail flapping,
hair flying.

My brother grabbed a board.
We lugged it up the windmill and ran it out
like a diving board under the old man's feet
and wedged our end below a crossbar. The old man
kept explaining, "I just climbed up to oil a squeak,
reached out to push the vane around, slipped, damn
puff of wind. I swung right out."

We felt strange helping him down.
In our whole lives, we never really held him before,
and now with his pants tangled around his feet
and him talking faster, getting hoarser
all the way down, explaining, explaining.

On solid ground, he quivered, pulling up his pants.
I said, "Good thing we came when we did."
His eyes burned from way back. His hands
were like little black claws. He spit Copenhagen
and words almost together. "Could have hung on
a long time yet. Anyway, you should have been home
half an hour ago."

HOW TO TAKE A WALK

This is farming country.
The neighbors will believe
you are crazy
if you take a walk
just to think and be alone.
So carry a shotgun
and walk the fence line.
Pretend you are hunting
and your walking will not
arouse suspicion.
But don't forget
to load the shotgun.
They will know
if your gun is empty.
Stop occasionally.
Cock your head and listen
to the doves you never see.
Part the tall weeds
with your hand and inspect
the ground.
Sniff the air as a hunter would.
(That wonderful smell
of sweet clover is a bonus.)
Soon you will forget
the gun in your hands,
but remember, someone
may be watching.

If you hear beating wings
and see the bronze flash
of something flying up,
you will have to shoot it.

LOST SOLITUDE

I have five daughters, who flowered like shadows.
I could have lived alone in my own cave,
but here they are wanting dresses and wallpaper.
Their slim arms harvest in panic every new fashion.

Girlish dreams trip me up; five blank faces
watch every escape road.

Sitting on the evening porch, snatching at mosquitoes,
I am almost back in my cave, when one small hand
becomes a half-moon hanging on my shoulder.

MY FATHER IN THE DISTANCE

You crossed the pasture to the cornfield.
I cultivated toward the end of the row
where you waited in your faded overalls,
your hand resting on a fence post.
Your hand, only once, had rested on my head,
while we stood at the parlor window
and watched sparrows hopping on the porch.
As the corn rows shortened between us,
I saw again man and boy photographed
on glass, framed in the window.

Your hand dropped from the post.
I thought you had come with new orders.
Go home and fix the well pump?
Grind some hog feed?
I stopped the tractor and climbed down.
We talked. Talked about how the cockleburs
were almost gone, how the field
looked greener after that last rain,
how the corn should be knee high
by the 4th of July—important things.

THE FARM KID IN TOWN

My town cousins are Boy Scouts.
Campfires and canoes
beat the hell out of 4-H.
I walk beans, chopping cockleburs.
Town kids see westerns
and hike the river bluffs.

It rains this Saturday,
so we come to town but can't stay
for the movie at the Dakota Theater.
I hang around out front, drooling
over the new show poster,
Randolph Scott leading the cavalry
against savage redskin hordes.

Then a redskin my own size stands
beside me, looks at Randolph Scott,
and says, "Hey, this looks good,"
the same as I would have said it,
that wonder and wish in his voice.

I wonder how it feels
liking a show when your side loses.
But the jeans on this boy's slim hips
look wild as buckskin.
I envy him for both his lives, a town kid
and an Indian.

I would go with him and be his
faithful companion and sidekick.
We would cheer together
at General Custer movies.

MOTHERHOOD

I wash dishes,
looking out the window
above the sink. The girls,
on the grass, dress
the cats in doll clothes.
The orange tomcat,
wearing a lacy red dress
and pink bonnet,
breaks from their arms
up into the mulberry tree.
His claws splinter off
flakes of bark.
The girls make their voices
sweet: "Here, Buttercup,
here, Buttercup." Buttercup
crouches on a limb.
The tight bonnet draws
his eyes back, narrow
like slits
in a savage mask.

A FIRST GRADER'S
COUNTRY SCHOOL LESSON

He remembers one day from his first grade year. It was winter. During the noon recess, Benny and the other big boys built an igloo in the far corner of the schoolyard. Benny took a candle and a hatchet and crawled inside. Benny's friends rounded up the little boys and made them crawl into the igloo, one at a time. Each came out looking frightened. His turn came, and he was kicked in the butt and pushed on all fours inside the snow cave. He found himself kneeling over a block of ice, where a candle flickered, stuck in a Dad's Root Beer bottle. Benny stood above him like a giant. Black shadows danced up on Benny's face as he raised the hatchet and said, "Are you loyal to Benny? Say it, I'm loyal to Benny."

He said it. "I'm loyal to Benny."

That night at supper his father asked, "What did you learn in school today?"

SUN GOING DOWN

Old dog, I'm done feeling guilty
that I cut off your back leg
last year with the mower.
You couldn't catch jackrabbits
when you had that leg,
so don't look at me
with sad eyes tonight.
I saw you this morning,
doing just fine with your ladylove,
the Petersons' collie.
A stumpy leg didn't crimp your style.
I know I turned the tractor
too fast and should have paid
more attention when the sickle bar
swung around, but remember, dog,
it could have been worse.

NO QUESTION

There was no question,
I had to fight Arnold Gertz
behind the high school that Friday.
All fall he kept throwing pool balls
at me in the rec room.

There was no question,
I was scared spitless at the mere sight
of his grimy fists and bull neck.
When we rolled on the cinders
and grappled and thumped each other,

there was no question,
I was actually winning
when the principal broke us up.
And when Arnold went hunting pheasants
on Sunday, everybody said,

there was no question,
he was a damn fool to climb through
a barbed wire fence with a loaded shotgun.
There were exactly eight of us guys
who were classmates of Arnold so,

there was no question,
I had to be one of the pall bearers,
even though I never liked Arnold,
never would have, but I was sorry
the accident happened,

there was no question,
and if he hadn't got himself shot,
I wonder if he finally would have let me alone.
There is no question,
I wonder about that.

THE BREEDING SEASON

I felt the cold of early fall that night.
The men let me go along to the hog house
to watch the breeding.
Benny had been seeing it for five years.
He said, "It's better
than listening to *The Lone Ranger.*"

The hog house smelled of dust and manure.
Fly specks covered the yellow light bulb,
and shadows sat like dragons in the corners.
Merle, the hired man, lifted the gate.
Benny chased a sow into the boar's pen.

Pa and Merle leaned over the pen.
They rested their arms on the top board
and folded their hands.
I turned a five-gallon pail upside down,
stood on it, and leaned my arms on the pen.
I put my hands together and looked at Pa
to make sure I was doing it right.

Merle lifted his leg over the pen,
kicked at the boar, turned him around.
The two hogs snorted, shoved each other
with their snouts.
The boar got up on his hind legs
over the front of the sow. Her head
was underneath his belly. Merle said,
"Whoa, boy, you're getting on the wrong end."

Then Pa was in the pen. He turned
the sow, and the hogs pushed each other.
The boar kept climbing on the front of the sow.
Benny named the boar Wrong End. "Come on,
Wrong End, do your stuff," he said.

I was cold and tired. I remember
the two pigs fighting again
and streams of dust in the light.
We walked to the house, the men talking
about hogs. My eyes were sandy and sleepy,
but I felt good,
proud of having learned so much.

ONE WINTER NIGHT

A farmer sits on a kitchen floor,
building a toy barn for his son.
The farmer uses wood
from peach boxes and apple crates
because it costs nothing.
He straightens the old nails
and hammers them into the barn,
explaining to the boy
how a ridgepole
will make the roof solid.
There's a blizzard outside,
the kitchen window looks black,
and snow grains brush against the glass.
The barn, made of free wood
that could easily split and splinter,
comes together strong
because of habits in the man's hands.
The son's barn on the kitchen floor
has the proportions and shape
of the man's huge red barn outside,
except that, on the small barn,
the man uses some gray paint
left from painting the porch floor
two summers ago.
He explains to the boy,
there is no leftover red paint,
and the boy, because he is the son
of this man,
knows that the logic of a gray barn
is perfect.

TORNADO

Aunt Cordelia was a tough old lady.
We could hardly believe
she was ever a little girl.
She told this story:

We stood on the porch and watched
the gray finger come down from clouds
in the west and dirt swirling up.
Mama said, "It's over Milo's place."
"No," Papa said, "it's farther south."
My little sister knew
that Mama and Papa were afraid.
Papa opened the outside cellar door
and herded us in. We stood crowded
on the top steps, watching that thing
in the west. Papa wasn't one to touch
us often, but now his hands hopped
like sparrows from one shoulder
to the next, making sure
we were all there. Even smarty pants
Benny kept his mouth shut.

The tail snaked out and swung around
to the south. Papa became his old self.
The next day, we piled in the car
to go see how bad the Knutson place
was wrecked. Papa said they were lucky
and all got into the cellar.

Benny said, "Pooh, if I got caught
outside in a tornado, I would just grab
a hold around a tree."
Papa smiled, but his face was fierce
and helpless, too.
We turned into Knutson's driveway
and saw big trees broken, twisted, and torn
out by the roots. Papa said, "Which tree
would you have hung on to?"

THE BOMB LADY VISITS
MAVIS MATSON

At first I thought
she was the Avon lady,
same color car.
I was digging parsnips,
the last thing living
in our garden,
a bad growing year.

I let her into my kitchen,
and we sat by the table.
She had a government job,
taking a survey—
did we have
a place to go if it
happened? A cellar.
Did we have
any food stockpiled?
Parsnips.

I thought the bomb lady
looked familiar.
Aren't you a Peterson?
My mother was.
Charley's girl?
Marlene's second cousin.
My yes, we are all
practically relatives.

I showed the bomb lady
the crocheted doily
I had finished yesterday.
We talked about ways
to make chokecherry jelly.

Parsnips and preserves
and our fires
banked against winter,
we are never amazed
enough that the green shoots
come from the damp ground
every spring.

THE AUCTION

Not even a bid
on the old plow
rusting in the grove.

We were married only months
when he took all our money
and bought that plow—

really all my money, money
I had earned as a hired girl,
babysitting, walking beans.

He didn't ask me,
just bought the plow.
Our first big fight.

His main fault maybe—
if something needed doing,
he didn't think about feelings.

I feel him behind me now.
He touches my shoulders in a way
that says he remembers

how much that plow cost.

COUNTRY CHURCH FIRST COMMUNION

They stood the first communion kids
on the bottom step, the steeple behind
almost touching the black clouds.
Wind tore at veils and lifted collars.
Mothers bent over cameras and fumbled
to get pictures before the rain.
The lightning flash and explosion
came together. Across the road,
a cottonwood tree split down the trunk
to the ground. Out of the silence,
Old Man Brunner muttered, "Ho-
ly shit." The rain splashed
on the gravel. They broke
for their cars, rough hands guiding
little girls in wet lace. The car doors
slammed, sounding cold and dangerous.

PART II ❋ OLD MAN BRUNNER

OLD MAN BRUNNER'S WALTZ

Old Man Brunner, black hair
plastered across his head,
comes to the dance wearing
brown pants, blue blazer,
green shirt, purple tie.
His cracked shoes are smeared
with Esquire liquid polish
right over the cow manure.
Around midnight,
some boys, barely old enough
to drink beer, full of envy,
watch Old Man Brunner dance
with a real woman.

Hey, would you look
at that: Old Man Brunner
waltzing with Selma Lund.
Some tight skirt, I'd like
to give her a whirl myself.
See how high he picks up
his feet and sets them down,
like he planned every step—
one, two, three,
with a little dip going into
the first step.
A woman like that, not even
half his age. His breath
must be all whiskey
and tobacco. Still,
the old buzzard can waltz.

OLD MAN BRUNNER SPEARING CARP
ON WOLF CREEK

Early spring, rushing water,
he is out there, below the bridge
at a narrow channel, poised
with a pitchfork. He spears, pitches
huge carp onto the bank,
where they flop and buck until dust
cakes on their green scales.
Old Man Brunner will drive
around to neighbors,
giving away carp from a wet gunnysack.
This is Old Man Brunner's gift,
the flesh of the carp,
his way of almost giving himself,
and there are still those who accept.

IF OLD MAN BRUNNER WERE GOD

Baling wire keeps the bumper
on Old Man Brunner's truck,
the muffler on his tractor.
Old Man Brunner can fix anything
with baling wire:
a wagon tongue, an iron gate,
a split seam in his overalls,
his reading glasses.
If Old Man Brunner had made
the world, baling wire coils
would spark the lightning
in the clouds. Baling wire
would keep the continents
from sinking, twisted strands
would hold the planets
in orbit. Baling wire
would grow like grass.
Old Man Brunner's universe
would be a rusty paradise
where anything could be fixed
with a pair of pliers.

OLD MAN BRUNNER IN CONTROL

Matson's black dog crouches in the grove, waiting to ambush Old Man Brunner's truck. The Dodge truck roars down the road. Old Man Brunner blows the horn. The dog goes crazy. He runs down the driveway and lopes out ahead of the truck, kicking gravel back at the windshield. Old Man Brunner chaws on his WB Cut and drools tobacco juice. "God damn dog." He swerves at the dog, but again the dog is too quick and veers off into the ditch.

Late one night, Old Man Brunner is driving home. He switches on the light in the truck cab and reaches for his pint of Seagram's 7. Coming up on the Matson place, Old Man Brunner doesn't even think of blowing the horn, but the dog is waiting anyway. He charges out but realizes too late that he has miscalculated. Half squatting, front legs stiff, the dog slides out in front of the truck.

The dog and man see astonishment in each other's faces. Old Man Brunner actually hits the brakes. "God damn dog." The bumper knocks the dog flat, the truck passes clean over him, then skids and bounces into the ditch. Old Man Brunner is down on the floorboards, his shoulder on the gas pedal. The truck roars along in the ditch. Old Man Brunner hooks an arm through the steering wheel and hauls himself onto the seat. Old Man Brunner is in control again, up on the next field driveway, back on the road. He touches a gash above his bushy eyebrow and reaches for his pint of whiskey. "God damn dog."

OLD MAN BRUNNER PLAYS HIS CARDS

We play pinochle at Old Man Brunner's kitchen table. The wood box is empty. Old Man Brunner finds part of an old tire someplace and stuffs it into the cookstove. We pour another round of Seagram's 7. The smell of burning rubber doesn't bother us. I am Old Man Brunner's partner. He lectures me after every hand. "Why the hell did you lead off your ace of trump? You knew I had the hundred aces. If you'd played your king, it would have forced Walter's ten, and we wouldn't have gone set by one."

The stove pipes glow red, and in spite of all the Seagram's 7, we worry some. Walter says, "I think the chimney's on fire."

"Deal the cards," says Old Man Brunner. We play another hand. I get another lecture. So far as anyone knows, Old Man Brunner has never made a mistake playing pinochle. I wish the house would catch fire so I might say, "If you wouldn't have put that tire in the stove, the chimney wouldn't have caught fire, and the house wouldn't have burned down."

But the house doesn't catch fire. I feel like Matson's black dog, who lies in wait every day to chase Old Man Brunner's truck. I wait for Old Man Brunner to make a mistake. He never does. And if he did, I probably wouldn't say anything. He'd just find a way out.

OLD MAN BRUNNER NAILS JESUS TO THE CROSS FOR WENDELL AND BERNICE

It started when Bernice found
an old crucifix in the junk room,
except there was no cross,
only a bronze Jesus with the nails
still through the hands,
and Bernice asked Old Man Brunner
to make another cross,
so two nights later he came to our place
with the cross ready for the Jesus,
and Old Man Brunner did a fine job,
I got to admit,
with some solid oak, real hard stuff,
from a chair leg,
and I told him he'd better
drill some holes first
or he'd never get those little nails
pounded into that hard wood,
but he wouldn't listen
and spent twenty minutes nailing
the Jesus to that cross,
and you know how religious Bernice
always was, and I could tell
it was all starting to bother her,
with Old Man Brunner hammering
on the kitchen table, and the nails
kept bending over

until they all broke off, so Bernice said,
let Wendell do it,
but it didn't seem like something
I wanted any part of,
and then Old Man Brunner was going to use
some shingle nails
he had in his pocket, but Bernice
wouldn't hear of that,
said it wouldn't look right, so I found
some tiny brass screws,
but Bernice said those wouldn't look right
either and they didn't even have screws
back in those days,
and Old Man Brunner made a joke
that I don't remember exactly, but it got
Bernice really mad,
but Old Man Brunner finally put the Jesus
on the cross and used the brass screws
anyway, but afterwards he took a file
and flattened out the screw heads,
so you couldn't tell them from nails.

OLD MAN BRUNNER ON HALLOWEEN NIGHT

We breathed the fresh night
into our young heads. Benny led us
through Old Man Brunner's grove
toward the dark shape
of Old Man Brunner's outhouse.
Our arms reached to push against
the back wall, and we fell.
The ground was gone. Old Man
Brunner had moved the toilet
three feet forward. In the pit,
we stumbled all over ourselves
while Old Man Brunner's shotgun
blasted the trees above our heads.
But the worst came later,
when Old Man Brunner told everyone
how he had played plenty of Halloween pranks
in his time and never would have fallen
for such a trick. I tried to picture
Old Man Brunner as a young man.
I could see only the stooped shoulders,
the hawk face, the beady eyes
and bushy eyebrows—Old Man Brunner,
with a sly grin, tipping toilets,
hoisting a cultivator on top
of a chicken coop. Old Man Brunner
dragging a hog up into a hayloft.

OLD MAN BRUNNER'S RUNAWAY HORSES

Old Man Brunner has his road ditch mowed.
He hitches his horses
to the hay rake and heads out the driveway.

There is nothing Old Man Brunner sees
that he can blame for spooking
those horses—maybe a bumblebee, maybe
a snake—but they're off, galloping
with Old Man Brunner yelling,
"Whoa, you sonsabitches."
Old Man Brunner is two feet above the seat
more than he is on it.

Matson's wife is out getting the mail.
She stands holding the mailbox door open,
her mouth open, then dives into the ditch.
Pages of the *Argus Leader* fly up
like a flock of big white birds.
Matson's black dog runs out barking
and is almost trampled.

Old Man Brunner finally stops the horses
and turns them into the ditch.
He rakes back toward home. Mavis Matson
climbs up on the other side
of the road as Old Man Brunner goes by.
"Are you all right?" she asks.

Old Man Brunner says, "I was going to start
down on this end anyway." He trips
the rake, dumping a pile of hay, and says
over his shoulder, "You ought to keep
that dog chained up."

OLD MAN BRUNNER AND THE TRAVELING SALESMAN

One stormy night a traveling salesman's car breaks down right by Old Man Brunner's driveway. The traveling salesman knocks on his door and asks for a place to sleep. Old Man Brunner is surprised and happy to find himself in a joke that he has told many times. "You're welcome to stay the night," he says, "but we're short on beds—you'll have to sleep with my daughter." (Old Man Brunner is a widower, and his children grew up and moved out long ago.)

The traveling salesman hesitates. He is actually thinking it over. Finally he says, "Oh, I can sleep in the car."

"Don't you want to see what she looks like?"

"I'll sleep in the car."

"It's all right," says Old Man Brunner. "She's out in the barn finishing chores."

He takes the arm of the traveling salesman and guides him to the barn. Old Man Brunner opens the door and switches on the light. "There she is," he says, pointing to a heifer in a pen.

"I'll sleep in the car," says the traveling salesman, turning and walking off into the rain.

Someone else, in Old Man Brunner's place, may have hoped for a better ending. But for Old Man Brunner, it is enough. He has a story he can tell to a whole lot of people.

OLD MAN BRUNNER SITS ON HIS PORCH

Old Man Brunner never cuts his weeds.
Right up to the house,
sunflowers and fire weeds
grow tough and hard as small trees.
In the summer evenings, Old Man Brunner
sits and surveys his jungle,
his sleeves rolled up,
his cracked shoes beside him.
Old Man Brunner's feet are white,
white as angel feet.
He holds one white foot in his brown hand
and cuts his toenails
with a tin shears.

OLD MAN BRUNNER'S CHICKENS

He'll have an egg for breakfast now and then.
At times he'll even kill a chicken, scald
and pluck it, fry it up, but otherwise
at Old Man Brunner's place, those chickens live
without much threat or help from him. They pick
up oats around the yard. At harvest time
they eat their fill, but mostly life is rough.
Raccoons and weasels get them. Still, a few,
the toughest ones, survive. They roost way up
on cottonwood tree branches, safe, except
for those that Old Man Brunner shoots right through
the head with his old, rusty twenty-two.
I know what Old Man Brunner means when he
says someone doesn't have a chicken's chance.

PART III ❀ WHAT MILO SAW

THE BELT BUCKLE

There's no use putting it off, Audrey,
I'll tell you straight out,
I can't make myself wear
that belt buckle you gave me.
It isn't true that I have looked
for a belt worthy of that buckle.
I haven't been looking. Audrey,
you might have bought a buckle
with anything else on it, a lone star,
for instance. A horse, a six-gun,
a saddle, a boot, or even one of those
blue Indian stones. But you had to buy
a belt buckle with, of all things,
the Praying Hands. I know
your intentions were good, Audrey,
but didn't you stop and think
what those hands would be praying over?
A man wearing that buckle in bars,
sooner or later, would have to fight.
I ask you, Audrey, would Willie Nelson
wear such a buckle? I hate to hurt
your feelings, Audrey. Maybe
I could hang it on my truck dashboard.

THE DEAD

There are graves in the east forty, out away from the trees. The graves were once marked by a clump of lilac bushes, which Uncle Carl dug out and plowed over. Old Carl kept his mouth shut, and when the neighbors started to talk, he pretended he didn't know that people were buried there, but everyone knew that Carl just didn't want to lift his plow and go around those lilacs. A man from the courthouse and the preacher came out. They said those graves had to be marked. "Look," Carl said, "why not put up your stone over next to the grove? We'll never find the right spot anyway."

"Then we'll have to dig until we find it," they said.

After the bulldozer turned over half an acre, Carl's memory improved. They dug up two skeletons that looked like a man and a child. Carl said, "As long as you have them dug up, why not bury them over close to the trees?"

But no, they said it would be disrespectful to move a grave.

THE NEW LADY BARBER
AT RALPH'S BARBERSHOP

She's in there all right,
cutting hair alongside Ralph.
From California, they say,
young, blonde, and built.
A woman has no business
being a barber, we said.
But soon we saw
how Old Man Brunner walked
back and forth
past the barbershop,
not going in until
somebody was in Ralph's chair
and hers was empty.
In a month we were all
glancing into Ralph's window,
timing our haircuts.
A woman has no business
being a barber, our wives say.
One thing is dead certain
in this town:
we will never have topless
dancers or massage parlors.
When strangers
ask what we do for excitement,
we can say we got a lady barber
if your timing is right.

DOREEN HAS ANOTHER RUMMAGE SALE

I told my missus,
No, I won't walk across the alley
to Doreen's rummage sale,
even if she is my sister.
Ever since Elmer died, Doreen
runs to every rummage sale
in town. She buys chairs
that look like the stuffing exploded,
pans not fit to feed a dog out of,
hats a horse wouldn't wear.
Doreen's yard is a bankrupt
salvage company, and now she plans
to turn a profit on junk no one else
was dumb enough to buy.

Well, Doreen goes into the house
and leaves her wobbly card table
and the cigar box that she figures
to fill with money by sundown.
I couldn't get mad when I saw the missus
sneak over and put a few dollars
in the cigar box. At least she
didn't bring home a plaster Chinaman
with a clock in his bellybutton,
like last time.

A FARM BOY REMEMBERS

Saturday was for cleaning barns,
forking out tons of manure.
There are more significant ways
to spend a Saturday, when the snow
is melting, but this was ours.
Throw out the shit
and put down clean straw.
Renewal has never since been so simple.

BENNY IN LOVE

Meadowlarks sing around the country schoolhouse. Benny has done nothing inventive for two weeks. The teacher worries. She remembers when Mrs. Himple, the county superintendent, visited the school. Benny made a tiny cardboard wagon. The wagon tongue was a strip of paper glued to the backs of four boxelder bugs. They pulled the wagon right to the feet of Mrs. Himple. But now Benny's imagination moves in new directions. Benny is in love with Eva Hofstader. He dreams about rescuing Eva Hofstader from peril.

Benny thinks about the notorious George Sitz, bank robber and killer, hiding in ditches, underneath bridges. Needing food, George Sitz comes to the schoolhouse. He waves his forty-five automatic at the teacher and makes her stand in a corner. Then George Sitz orders the kids against the wall. George Sitz grabs Eva Hofstader's arm and forces her to collect the lunch boxes.

George Sitz sits in a first grader's front desk and gobbles sandwiches as fast as the terrified Eva Hofstader can open lunch boxes. Above his head hangs the world globe from a cord that goes up over a pulley. The cord runs across the ceiling, over another pulley, and down along the wall, where it is tied to an iron ball the size of a baseball. You can raise and lower the globe, and it stays where you leave it because the iron ball weighs the same as the globe. Benny works his way behind the little kids to the wall. He sneaks out his Swiss pocketknife and cuts the cord. The world crashes down on George Sitz's head. Benny grabs the iron ball, charges out, and conks him again to make sure. Eva Hofstader throws her arms around Benny's neck. Benny lets her hug him for awhile. Then he ties up George Sitz with the globe cord.

Day after day, Benny thinks through the rescue of Eva Hofstader, refining the details. He feels her chest against him, her face warm on his neck. He smells her clean brown hair. But then the sheriff captures George Sitz. George Sitz will probably get the electric chair. Benny finally starts work on his science project for the county fair.

One morning the teacher finds the smoking remains of a fried mouse in Benny's electric mousetrap.

THE PRINCE

Charlene walks through the grove,
picking daisies. She sits,
leaning against a cottonwood tree,
weaves herself a flower crown,
closes her eyes, and dreams
of Robert Redford on a horse
come to take her away.

Charlene wakes to a clattering engine.
It's Marvin Ackerman, the neighbor boy,
on a John Deere tractor,
cultivating corn. Marvin grins
and waves wildly. He will probably ask
her out again. She is thinking
she might as well say yes.

AFTER FORTY YEARS OF MARRIAGE, SHE TRIES A NEW RECIPE FOR HAMBURGER HOTDISH

"How did you like it?" she asked.

"It's all right," he said.

"This is the third time I cooked
it this way. Why can't you
ever say if you like something?"

"Well if I didn't like it,
I wouldn't eat it," he said.

"You never can say that anything
I cook tastes good."

"I don't know why all the time
you think I have to say it's good.
I eat it, don't I?"

"I don't think you have to say
all the time it's good, but once
in a while you could say
you like it."

"It's all right," he said.

FARM WIFE

The last pan
from the silent noon meal
is washed and back
in the cupboard, and he
is back in the field.

She looks through
the window at fences
patched with rusted wire
and splintered stakes
driven into hard ground.
The dusty trees are quiet
under the force of heat.

She lies down on the couch
in the shade-drawn parlor.
The silence glaring outside
closes around and waits.

BACHELOR

Too much
apricot brandy.
I can see
how I live,
a two-room shack,
peeling wallpaper,
dirty quilts,
rusty sink.
I know the joke
they tell
about the mattress
I ordered
from the Sears
and Roebuck catalog.
They say I thought
that the woman
on the mattress
was included.
But by God,
I might go
and court
Henry's widow.
She might be
my last chance.

WHAT MILO SAW

We worried about our neighbor Milo.
After the hail pounded his corn crop
into the ground, Milo said
he would shoot himself. Milo's wife raved.
She cried into her greasy apron and worried.
Milo's six runny-nosed kids were scared quiet
for a change. Milo took his beat-up
Chevy truck and ran off to town
twice a week and got drunk. Late at night,
on the way home, Milo somehow kept the Chevy
between the fences.

The drought came and dried up Milo's pasture.
Milo was down to his last cow.
He got drunk three times a week and still
managed to keep the Chevy between the fences,
but one night he scraped the machine shed
door a little and tore off a fender.
Milo said he would shoot himself.
Milo's wife hid the shotgun in the cellar
on a shelf, behind the pickle jars.

One day Milo's old watering tank fell apart.
Milo and the six kids dragged an old bathtub
out of the grove so that the one last cow
would have a place to drink.
Milo drove the beat-up Chevy to town.

The next morning, Milo found the one last cow
drowned in the bathtub—flat on her back, legs
sticking straight up, milk bag and tits
sort of floating just under the water.

Years later, Milo told somebody, if a man
was going to kill himself, just show him
a drowned cow in a bathtub.

A FARMER PRAYS

My bank loan overdue,
that tractor I bought
had a cracked block.
Lord, you know
I'd never wish anyone dead,
but when the time is up
for that bandit
John Deere dealer,
let him be showing off
a new manure spreader.
Let him fall
into the beaters
and be spread
over half the township,
amen.

DISCUSSION AT THE WOLF CREEK STORE

"If we went back a couple hundred years, came up the Missouri River with Lewis and Clark, could we leave the boat and find the places our farms are on right now?"

"No landmarks for a man to go by, all grass and rolling hills."

"I'd find the James River, where it runs into the Missouri, travel north, say, one good day on horseback, look for the highest ground, come back one mile south and two west. Wouldn't that work?"

"Hell no!"

"Who knows?"

"Listen, if we could go back a couple hundred years and had any sense, we wouldn't be looking for the places we got now."

FARMING THE HIGH SCHOOL HOMECOMING

Okay, let's suppose for a minute
that nothing in the float building
and parade was worth remembering.
And suppose we were
fooling ourselves, thinking
that for once we had something
over the town kids because we
had the flatbed wagons and the chicken wire.
Maybe there was
nothing original in our themes for floats:
a paper heart and a treasure chest
under the words—TIGERS THE TREASURE
OF OUR HEARTS. Or a boat
mounted on a flatbed—SAILING TO VICTORY.
Or the theme we really wanted,
which the girls vetoed, a giant crepe paper
jock strap—LET THIS NOT BE OUR ONLY SUPPORT.
Suppose there is nothing really important
in all that, and there probably isn't
(our papier-maché usually crumbled).
Still, we were never in danger
of believing we could cover our plainness
with ceremony and tin foil.
The warm October wind
always whipped in from the country and blew
the pastel Kleenexes clean
out of the chicken wire, exposing
old manure stains on the flatbed tires.

CORN POEM

I don't mind it so much being a corn-
fed corn ball sitting here by the corn-
crib, smoking corn silk in a corn-
cob pipe, playing a cornet, sipping corn
whiskey, and eating Doritos corn
chips. But where, where is my corn-
ucopia? When will I walk in tall corn?

PART IV ❀ DRINKING THE MOON

A CLEAR DAY

My field is harrowed and ready.
We eat breakfast while Donna's wash water
heats in a copper tub on the cookstove.
Musty clothes spill from cardboard boxes
scattered around the kitchen.

Outside, I smell the bright cold
and bitter wood smoke. I do not fall
on my knees, clutching fistfuls of soil
to my chest. A spring wind chills
worse than winter. Last year's brittle
corn leaves drift over the field
like scraps of yellow paper.

I turn up my collar and start planting
again, pouring oat seed from gunnysacks
into the drill boxes, making that first run
along the fence line, watching
the face of my field change.

DEATH CEREMONY

The neighbors dug his grave,
twenty farmers for a two-man job
and enough shovels to bury death itself.
Old Man Brunner's truck made two runs
to the Wolf Creek Store for beer.

The men lounged against tombstones,
chewed grass stems, felt dizzy
in the sunshine. Old Man Brunner kept
saying, "I tell you, you got
the bottom of the hole farther north
than the top—she doesn't go straight
down." When they corrected the slant,
the grave was almost square.
Everyone had a turn at digging.

And neighbors pitching in almost got
the best of death. But one man, then
another, looked away to the south, squinting
into an eye-watering wind blowing sweet
over the waving grass—the last field
of prairie hay in Willow County.

THE WORD MAN

No one knew where Johnson's hired man
had been before. We thought he was an Indian,
but his hair was red. He used strange words
that Johnson couldn't even find in the dictionary.
The hired man's name was Copernicus Smith,
but the kids called him The Word Man.

Copernicus said, "The weather looks *larkuler*
today." And, "The tractor runs like a *nukeflee*
this morning." He used his words on animals, too.
They seemed to understand better than people.
He said, "You cats will *wabagatch* when I'm around."
Once when Copernicus was tying up a cow in the stall,
he whispered in her ear, "The bull *grovalates*
when you are in the pasture." Johnson swears
the cow couldn't wait to get out of the barn.

People asked questions: "What does *slow-waft* mean?"
Copernicus said, "*Slow-waft* means something like
drawflutter." "Where do you get all these words?"
"They come from the *vu-carple* part of the brain."

Kids liked Copernicus and started using his words.
Arguments started in school: "*Sluseroo* means someone
who is dumb." "No, *sluseroo* is when two pigs kiss."
But the teacher worried. Some of the words sounded
dirty. Benny, the eighth grader, told Alice Bertleson
to go *grovalate* herself.

One Sunday afternoon, the teacher and the mothers
visited Johnson's and had a talk with Copernicus.
Copernicus said that he didn't want to *semepolate*
any trouble. Johnson was sorry to lose Copernicus—
he was a good worker.

THE CLASS REUNION DANCE

I dance with the woman
no one danced with back then
when she was broomstick skinny
and broken out in pimples.
She's beautiful now and married
to a North Dakota wheat farmer.

This is more than I deserve,
her cheek against my shoulder
as we dance
a slow sentimental journey
around the gym, acting as though
we have something to recover.

When the music stops,
we tell each other, Thanks,
and we both seem happy.
The wheat farmer frowns a little.

THE RETURN OF SPRING

I walk across the cattle yard,
looking above the mud
at the trees. My boot sticks,
and I pull my foot out.

I balance like a dancer
on one leg, the other leg curved
gracefully, back arched,
arms spread like wings, chest out.

I hold that elegant pose
and watch three crows gliding
around the tips
of branches sprouting buds.

The moon-eyed cows stand still,
envying my grace, and I know
I'm never going to get my foot
back into that boot.

BEHIND THE PLOW

I look in the turned sod
for an iron bolt that fell
from the plow frame
and find instead an arrowhead
with delicate, chipped edges,
still sharp, not much larger
than a woman's long fingernail.
Pleased, I put the arrowhead
into my overalls pocket,
knowing that the man who shot
the arrow and lost his work
must have looked for it
much longer than I will look
for that bolt.

CORN-GROWING MUSIC

In that hazy stillness
between summer and fall,
they say you can hear
corn grow. Leaves stir
and sing a whispering song.

I look over my field
and want to conduct
my million-stalk chorus.
I could wave my arms
like a lunatic—louder,
louder, you bastards,
I still owe the bank
for your seed.

I listen again as leaves
flutter down the rows.
Maybe each stalk sings
its own growing song,
as I sing mine, or maybe
it's only the wind.

CLOSING IN ON THE HARVEST

No one could stop him.
A bad heart, he still
worked in the field
and said he would die
on the tractor.
Out on the Super-M
picking corn, somehow
he got off, though,
and sat on the ground,
leaning against the tire,
where we found him.
His eyes were wide open,
looking mean as hell,
like when he was alive
and chores weren't done,
but his hand
lay on his chest, gentle,
making us think
he was pledging something.
We could smell
the dry wind.
The tractor radio was on
to the World Series—
Cardinals 7, Yankees 5,
Bob Gibson on the mound,
one out to go—
the steel corn wagon
was not quite full.

BECOMING THE ANIMALS

He was a farmer who thought
his daydreams were foolish
but he still had daydreams,
and in them
he wanted to be his animals.
He rounded his shoulders
and bent over, shaping himself
like a four-hundred-pound hog
in a rye patch, listening,
wondering how a human hog call
would sound in floppy hog ears.
He wanted to be a Holstein cow
who needed his human hands
touching her flanks
at milking time. Most of all
he wanted to be a horse
and carry and ride himself
out of himself and back again.

ONE SEPTEMBER AFTERNOON

Home from town
the two of them sit
looking over what they have bought
spread out on the kitchen table
like gifts to themselves.
She holds a card of buttons
against the new dress material
and asks if they match.
The hay is dry enough to rake,
but he watches her
empty the grocery bag.
He reads the label
on a grape jelly glass
and tries on
the new straw hat again.

PLOWING AT FULL MOON

The air cold,
the hills roll up like unbroken
swells beneath the tractor,
the plow turning a wake
wet and black.

A column of fire gusts
up from the exhaust, the roar
breaks through
finally to a silence felt
in the hands and shoulder blades.

I am with the earth and the dark,
alone. And work is being done.
I'll go home and dream of a horse
bowing over still water in a cedar tank,
drinking the moon.

Hogs and Personals

PART I ❀ DROPPING THE PLOW

COULD YOU WRITE A FEW WORDS ABOUT WHAT YOU DID SINCE GRADUATION FOR THE HIGH SCHOOL ALUMNI NEWSLETTER?

Thirty years ago,
after we marched in the gym
and partied in the Legion Hall,
with the eastern sky lighting up,
I lay down on the back seat of my car
behind Maggie's Truck Stop Cafe.
No sense in getting home
just in time to milk the cows.
But I was too keyed up for sleep.
There was a box of dirty clothes
in the trunk, and I put on
a blue work shirt and jeans.
At the counter in Maggie's,
I ordered eggs, sunny side up.
A new waitress—I think
I noticed then for the first time
that a woman over thirty
could be sexy—asked if I
was going to work with the road
crew out west. "Yes," I lied.
Life on the highway seemed better
than going back to the farm.
"More coffee, honey?" she said.
"Sure, babe," I said. "What time
 you get off work?"
"Five this afternoon," she said,
 sounding as though
 she might not be kidding.

Skipping ahead a few years,
I can honestly say it's been
a good life, but never better
than that morning, driving home,
the car windows wide open,
and smells of spring grass blowing in.
The radio blared the latest hit,
"The Battle of New Orleans," a happy song
about war, and I sang along,
taking easy victory for granted.

INTO AND OUT OF DREAMS

Evening comes on hot and damp.
Tomorrow I need to cultivate corn,
and I hate this crazy idea my wife got
of going to some old movie.

2

In the night I dream
about lying under the tractor,
fixing a cultivator shank.
Marilyn Monroe, in the black and white
of the movie, hands me tools.
"Crescent wrench," I say.
"Crescent wrench," she whispers.
"Crescent wench," I say.

3

In the cool morning, I work
under the tractor while the wind
rustles the cottonwood leaves above.
I'm wearing clean overalls and a fresh
chambray shirt. I never could
carry a tune but find myself singing.
My wife, on her way to feed chickens,
stops and sets down her pail of oats.
"Please hand me that Crescent wrench,"
I say. "Crescent wrench coming up,"
she says, smiling down the length
of her body in full color.

FARMING IN A LILAC SHIRT

I opened the Sears catalog.
It was hard to decide—dress shirts
were all white the last time
I bought one, for Emma's funeral.
I picked out a color called *plum,*
but when the shirt arrived,
it seemed more the color of lilacs.
Still, it was beautiful.
No one I knew had a shirt like this.

After chores on Sunday, I dressed
for church. Suddenly the shirt
seemed to be a sissy color,
and I held it up near the window.
In the sun the lilac looked more lilac,
more lovely, but could a man
wear a shirt that color? Someone
might say, "That's quite the shirt."
I wore the old shirt to church.

And every Saturday night I thought,
Tomorrow I'll wear the shirt.
Such a sad terrible waste—to spend
good money on a shirt, a shirt
I even liked, and then not wear it.
I wore the shirt once, on a cold day,
and kept my coat buttoned.

In spring I began wearing the shirt
for everyday, when I was sure
no one would stop by. I wore the shirt
when I milked the cows and in the field
when I planted oats—it fit perfectly.
As I steered the John Deere,
I looked over my shoulder and saw
lilac against a blue sky
filled with white seagulls
following the tractor, and not once
did I wipe my nose on my sleeve.

AN OLD DANISH WOMAN

Her specialty is cinnamon rolls.
The scent of apple mixed with caramel goo
comes wafting from her little stucco house
across the street and meets me on the porch.
I might as well go over right away.
Her door will open any minute now.
"The coffee's on, come have a cup," she'll say.
When the diabetes came, she went right on
and made for others gifts she could not have
herself. I sit in her kitchen. Coffee steams
in plain white mugs. The rolls are there.
The rolls are always there. She puts one on
a plate and slides it over to me. She sips
her coffee, glances sideways, and I know
she's watching my face for some sign
of pleasure. "Good," I say. "Just wonderful."
She tears a sliver from a roll in the pan
and nibbles. There's a half glow in her face.
"I'd like to eat a whole roll," she says.

NIGHT VISION

In twilight I help the boys
pitch their blue dome tent
next to the grove behind the house,
more than enough wilderness
for their first time camping.
At midnight I sit on the bed,
staring at a shoe in my hand,
imagining silly dangers—a wolf
appears at the window,
grinning wickedly. Tomorrow
I will be found guilty
of carelessly going to sleep
while a beast devoured my children.
So I walk outside, where
the wet grass chills my feet.
Those black elm trees that lean
over the tent look like giant bears
that could be jolly or dangerous.
The boys took flashlights to bed.
Giggling stars swirl in galaxies
on the tent dome—a universe
that I see from the outside.

DREAMS WITHIN DREAMS

Deep in the night the same dream
comes back: I'm trying to farm again.
With enormous bank loans,
I've bought the seed corn,
machinery, livestock, tools,
but as I'm about to drop my plow
into the old fall stubble,

the nightmare part begins:
I realize it's all a mistake,
but instead of just walking away,
I plow the field, plant the corn,
pray for rain, go through the motions,
sad seasons stretching out ahead.
I faintly sense that it is a dream,

when suddenly, I'm driving a horse,
a trotter, around on a dark track.
The horse keeps breaking stride,
stumbling, stopping. I get off,
look into his face, and know

I'm in the dream of a horse
who was once a failure in harness.
I loosen his collar and keep my arms
around his neck—he stands still
accepting my embrace, and I can tell
he has lost a lot of races.

I stay with him for a long time,
his head breathing near mine,
while we both try hard to awaken.

FARMING WORDS

Once a farmer painted the word *cow*
on the sides of all his cows
so that deer hunters
would not mistake them for deer.
Then he discovered,
when he looked out over the pasture,
if he closed his eyes halfway
and squinted just right,
he could make the cows disappear,
and he saw only the words.
The farmer was delighted
as he watched the words move
and arrange themselves in lines
reaching off to the horizon.
He painted words on his other animals:
pig, hen, horse, sheep.
Before long, he did nothing but sit
on his porch all day and squint,
watching his words eat and mate.
He was never any good at real farming,
and this was more fun anyway.
But one day the farmer noticed
some words lying flat on the ground,
dead words. Other words just dried up.
Words ran away.
It was a bad year for words.
There was massive word failure.

VISIT TO A COUNTRY CEMETERY

The air of early fall smells dry.
Late prairie flowers bloom
along the fence. And here I am,
Mother, fresh from the barbershop.
I remember those sad Saturday nights
long ago, a dirty dishtowel pinned
around my neck. Your clipper caught
and pulled like a pair of pliers.
There was no answer I could give
in school when Bart McCoy asked
where the hell I got my haircuts.

I hope you haven't offered
to cut Jesus' hair.
I can see Him, though, seated
on a kitchen stool among the clouds
with you behind Him, clipping away.
Bits of His glorious locks fall
on His white robe and down His neck.
The old sorrow returns to His face
when you nick places
still sensitive from the thorns,
but He probably won't complain.

THE WIDOW LEAVES THE HOME PLACE

Our life had no sudden tragedy.
The kids grew up and left one by one,
and a slow cancer killed my husband.
People remember a barn that burns down
but forget a dozen that weather away.
I'm used to seeing deserted farms—
I never thought ours would be one.
Leaving would be easier if a new family
were moving onto the place.
I can imagine decayed gray boards,
broken windows, and tall yellow grass
up to the sills, but I can't bear
thinking about the years of dusty silence
that will settle in here.
So I have decided: before I leave
I'm going to cook dinner—fried chicken,
mashed potatoes, fresh bread, peas,
cucumbers, strawberries and cream.
I'll set the table the way I did
twenty-five years ago, fill the plates,
pour the coffee, and then I'll go.
Let whoever comes wonder,
What happened here? Why did they leave
so suddenly in the middle of a feast?
Let the detectives search for clues,
something out of place,
like a butcher knife stuck in the door,
where life was always ordinary
with never a sign of violence.

WHAT A CAT CAN DO IN KATMANDU

The meanest barn flies of the summer buzz
around my head, and sweat runs down my back.
I put the milker on the fourteenth cow.
The radio plays the saddest country song.
My six cats aren't underfoot but sprawled
in a corner. We're bored with our lives.
The music stops for the five o'clock news,
and things are happening in Katmandu.
This Katmandu sounds magic, like the name
of a jazz saxophone player or
a mountain pleasure palace. I begin
to chant softly, Katmandu, Katmandu.
The cats perk up. They recognize the word.
Yes sir, cats, Katmandu is where it's at.
Here you crawl around all day in a road ditch
for one scrubby gopher—in Katmandu
they'll serve you lightly poached goldfinch,
the feathers removed. The hotels have
green velvet rooms. World travelers rave
about the cathouses of Katmandu.
I say we split for Katmandu. Just drop
it all, get on that long road for Nepal,
because a cat can do in Katmandu
what a cat can't do in South Dakota.

PART II ❀ ANOTHER WARM FRONT

THE CURE

Sherill Ann takes my hand
in both of hers, looks
at the wart, and says
I got it from touching a toad.
I don't even remember
the last time I saw a toad,
but I like Sherill Ann
holding my hand, and I say,
Yes, it must have been
that toad I caught yesterday.
Sherill Ann says milk
from a milkweed will cure
the wart, which I don't believe,
but I meet her after school
in the pasture
behind the schoolhouse.
She breaks off the stem
of the milkweed,
applies the milk,
and then kisses me.
Soon the wart goes away.
I spend most of my time now
looking for toads.

A PRIVATE MATTER

I'm through going out with Kermit Walters.
Sunday afternoon we're parked
in his crummy Chevy under the cottonwood
behind the Dairy Queen, and he stirs
his milkshake with the straw and looks up
far away over the cornfield
and gets a silly smile on his face.
Then I ask why he's smiling, and he says
he just remembered something funny
that happened long ago,
but he won't tell me what it was.
I ask him why the hell he won't tell me.
He says it would take too long,
you had to be there, and most likely
it wouldn't be funny to anyone but him,
so I should just forget it.
Then I say I'm not so sure he wasn't laughing
at me or about something he doesn't dare
tell me, and I want him to know
that only an unbalanced person
goes around laughing to himself,
so he better tell me what's so damn funny.
He takes his comb out of his shirt pocket,
makes a couple of swipes through his hair
on both sides and combs it together in back.
He says it's a private matter
and reaches over and dumps what's left

of his strawberry milkshake
down the neck of my sweater, and laughs,
like that was supposed to be funny
or something.

SPRING

I'm watching Kay,
who's walking down the sidewalk,
watching her own reflection
in the windows
of Rexall Drugs, Ben Franklin,
and Pete's Pool Hall.
The June sky is bright blue,
and I can't help it, I'm in love
with Kay, who doesn't know
I'm watching her
watch her own reflection
in Beatrice's Beauty Salon,
the Rock Spring Saloon,
and Coast to Coast Hardware.
At first Kay doesn't notice me
because she's too busy
watching herself walking,
drawing her shoulders back,
and fluffing her blonde hair,
but then she stops and turns,
giving me her window smile
made perfect with practice.

THE BURDEN OF THE MUSE
IN A SMALL TOWN

On Saturday evening,
as usual, I'm sitting
on Irene's couch
in her apartment above
Dwyer's Hardware Store,
watching the fuzzy screen
of her black and white TV.
I'm about to open
my second bottle of Grainbelt,
when Irene says,
"I wish you'd say something witty
and romantic for a change."

What does she expect?
Poetry on demand?
I still have some good lines
left in me, but I'm tired—
it's the dog days of summer.
But I find myself
rummaging through my head,
thinking about the only
creative contribution
this town ever made
to the English language.
Word got around that Vernon,
who sang in a barbershop quartet,

was always telling his wife
that he was going to Sioux Falls
for singing practice.
"Singing Practice" became
the standard expression, as in
"My tomcat was out last night
at singing practice."

I set my beer down, turn to Irene,
put one hand above my heart,
unfold my other arm in a grand
sweeping gesture, and say,
"Irene, the corn chips
may have no snap left
and the Grainbelt
has lost most of its fizz,
but Irene, I
am ready for singing practice.
I need to break out
into song. Irene, let's see
if we can duet in close harmony.
One singing practice will bring
my warble to crooning perfection."
And Irene says, "Ha,
you can't even carry a tune."

THE LOVE NEST

Well, I don't care, Denise,
if you didn't win
the Dairy Princess Pageant.
By the time we're married
next spring, the new house
on the farm will be finished,
with a double garage
for your car and my pickup.
We'll panel the basement
with walnut veneer or maple
and tear down the old house
when my old man moves to town.
There'll be a new steel barn
and another Harvestore silo.
You know as well as I do,
Denise, you could hardly ask
for a better deal.
You're beautiful, Denise,
and I think if I bit
into your shoulder right now,
you'd taste like watermelon.

SECOND HONEYMOON IN A MOTEL
IN HOT SPRINGS, SOUTH DAKOTA

I wish he could forget
the hogs and worrying
about the boys handling
the milking machine.
It's the first time
we've slept away from home
in twenty years,
and he sits there reading
cattle prices in the paper
and watching weather on TV.
Does he remember what
they wrote years ago
on our wedding car,
"Hot Springs tonight"?
Can't he see now
a second warm front
moving in?

SLOWING DOWN THE TRAFFIC

Sometimes I still have it on my mind.
A year ago last spring, I hitched the disc
behind the tractor, and pulled onto the road.
It's a wide machine and a narrow stretch
of county blacktop—cars can't pass until
I reach the field a quarter-mile away.
A woman driving a white convertible,
with California plates, came up fast
behind me, almost rear-ended my rig.
She had enough blonde hair for a shampoo
commercial, full red lips, a perfect suntan.
Her sunglasses made her face mysterious,
a touch of glamour from a far-off place.
I found myself lifting my seed corn cap,
my fingers combing my sweaty hair
and smoothing stubble of day-old beard.
I drove full throttle, thinking, I suppose,
my huge machine and masterful control
somehow would impress her. So I swung
into the field and lifted my hand to wave.
I saw her face, impatient, hard, but still lovely,
as she gunned her car and gave me the finger.

CLASSIFIED: HOGS AND PERSONALS

Registered Hampshire Boar.
Rugged, productive.
Heavy-muscled,
but sensitive.
Loves to lounge
on fresh bedding
and listen to radio.
Eclectic musical tastes:
classical, especially Bach,
jazz and Willie Nelson.
Super-sound body.
Appealing belly contours.
Handsome classic snout.
Gentlemanly disposition,
but roots with roguish gusto.
Stands ready to clean up
any garbage in habitat.
Can show charm nonverbally.
Has engaging grunt.
Performance-tested.

PART III ❊ MY CRACKER JACK LIFE WITH ARLO

THE CRACKER JACK REWARD

In first grade Arlo won't color nice
so Miss Schraug sets a box of Cracker Jacks
up on the piano, for him when he learns
to stay inside the lines, but Arlo makes
a few Crayola scribbles on each picture in
his coloring book, and those Cracker Jacks
sit on the piano, getting stale all year.
I always color nice and never get a thing
for it. Then on the last day of school
Miss Schraug gives Arlo the Cracker Jacks
anyway, I suppose because he's cute,
and walking home from school, he gives me one
little handful and eats the rest himself.

ARLO SHOWS GOOD SENSE

Halfway through the dry summer
before we start high school,
when farm work slacks off,
Arlo's uncle hires us to clean out
the cellar of his paint store.
To let in light, we clean years
of dirt from the windows,
discovering we can look
up through one window,
through the sidewalk grate
on Main Street, and see
up the dresses of women.

We wait for Juanita Sanders,
the dentist's receptionist,
new in town, young, dark-haired,
and divorced. There are rumors
she doesn't wear panties.

Arlo and I see little more
than blurs of flesh and shadows,
but we learn that Juanita
wears canary yellow panties.
We get the idea of sneaking
into the dentist's office
at noon, when she's out for lunch,
and leaving a note on her desk.

I write on a sheet of brown
wrapping paper, "That's a lovely pair
of yellow panties you have on today."
But Arlo thinks maybe we better
forget it, and when I ask why,
he just shrugs. I crumple the note
and throw it in the trash can.

In September, when I go
to get my teeth cleaned,
I feel uneasy in the waiting room,
but Juanita hardly notices me.
She is beautiful, mysterious,
and untouchable, answering
the phone, filing her nails,
and reading a paperback book
called *Breakfast at Tiffany's*.

I picture Juanita reading
the brown paper note she never saw.
Her eyes glance around nervously,
losing all their mystery.
At night she looks out of her windows,
afraid that someone is watching.
I'm thankful that Juanita
wears panties and that Arlo
sometimes has good sense.

FISHING

We have caught nothing, fishing all day
for bluegills in the Wolf Creek Dam,
when Arlo hooks and hauls in a carp,
big as a young hog. On the way home,
we decide to show the fish
to the Peterson sisters—we'll use
any excuse to visit Charlene and Yvonne,
who are in the yard, carrying buckets
of skim milk to feed the pigs.

Yvonne always makes me feel
a warm ache all over, especially now,
in her pink shorts smudged with dirt
and sweat-stained halter top.
I want to caress the bright red scratch
on one of her luscious thighs.

Arlo bends over the trunk of the Ford,
lifts out the carp, cradled in his hands,
and shoves its head toward the girls.
They squeal and jump back a step.
Arlo says that carp are a friendly fish—
their lips are in the shape of a kiss.
Arlo says he'll give Yvonne a quarter
if she will kiss the carp. Yvonne says, "Yuk."
"Come on, Yvonne," he says, "kiss the carp.
Fifty cents, Yvonne, just kiss the carp.

One dollar, Yvonne, please, kiss the carp."
And then Yvonne leans forward, balanced
on her dainty tiptoes, her arms drawn back,
showing off her breasts, and those precious,
pouty lips touch the lips of the wet fish.

Yvonne tells Arlo to pay up. He tosses
the carp into the trunk and shows her
the empty pocket of his plastic billfold.
Yvonne says, "Oh, you," and pounds his chest,
but not hard. Arlo grabs her shoulders,
and they fall, laughing and wrestling
on the grass beside the yard light pole.
It's ridiculous. I would have paid Yvonne
a dollar to kiss me. I've got
to hand it to Arlo though—sometimes
he really has a way with women.

GAINING YARDAGE

The word *friend* never came up
between Arlo and me—we're farm neighbors
who hang around together, walk beans,
pick rocks, and sit on the bench
at football games, weighing the assets
of the other side's cheerleaders.
Tonight we lead 48 to 6, so the coach
figures sending us both in is safe.
I intercept an under-thrown pass
only because I'm playing the wrong position,
and Arlo is right there to block for me
because he's in the wrong place.
We gallop up the field, in the clear
until their second-string quarterback
meets us at the five-yard line,
determined to make up for his bad throw.
Arlo misses the block, the guy has me
by the leg and jersey, and going down,
I flip the ball back to Arlo, getting up,
who fumbles, and their quarterback
almost recovers, then bobbles the ball
across the goal line, and our coach,
who told even the guys with good hands
never to mess around with laterals,
must feel his head exploding,
when Arlo and I dive on the ball together
in the end zone and dance and slap
each other on the back.

They give Arlo the touchdown, which rightly
should be mine, but I don't mind,
and I suppose we are friends, and will be,
unless my old man or his decides to move
to another part of the country.

ARLO AND I WRESTLE
FOR THE LAST TIME

I outweigh him by ten pounds
and usually have a slight edge,
but this Saturday afternoon
we seem evenly matched.
In the barn at his place, we roll
around on the hayloft floor.
Every time I think I have him
in a good hold, he slips free.
The early winter darkness
begins creeping into the barn.
I should be home, starting chores.
Finally, I straddle his chest
and get his arm in a figure-four lock.
I doubt he can escape
but don't know for sure.
After five minutes,
I let him go and walk away.
"Are you chicken?" he shouts.
I don't turn around,
not wanting to look at his dusty,
sweat-streaked face again,
and I walk the quarter-mile home.

But after supper I am happy
to see his rusty '49 Ford
drive into the yard. He cranks

the window down and asks
if I want to go along into town
and shoot some pool or go to the show,
maybe pick up a couple of broads.
"Sure," I say, rubbing my forearms.
"My arms still ache."
"Yeah," he says, "mine, too. All
that gripping each other causes it."

THE SPACE BETWEEN

Arlo and I walk the bean rows,
chopping sunflowers and cockleburs.
Through the morning, we talk
about fishing, Minnesota Twins baseball,
and Yvonne Peterson's breasts.
But in the hot afternoon, we stop talking.
Our feet are heavy with dirt
caked on our shoes. I notice that Arlo
has stopped chopping weeds in the space
between his four rows and mine.
In the morning, sometimes he chopped
the weeds in that space, sometimes I did.
It wasn't something we had to discuss,
but now he takes no responsibility
for that area. I lag a few steps back.
There's a six-foot sunflower
in the middle of that no man's land,
and Arlo marches right by.
I suppose I could say, "I'll take care
of that space going up the field
and you get it coming back."
But some things shouldn't need
spelling out. So I'm stuck with all
the weeds between us, but since
we've finished the worst part of
the field, they don't amount to much.

THE ART OF HOG BUTCHERING

Arlo tells me to think about
the money we'll save on meat,
now that we both are married
with kids on the way.
We saw our fathers do this,
so we're teeming with confidence,
acting as if we've slaughtered hogs
our whole lives, discussing methods—
whether to shoot the hog or use
a sledge hammer, whether to scald
and scrape the hog or skin it.

We should have started earlier.
At noon in Arlo's barn, the hog
lies on its back, half skinned, a maze
of baling twine strung from the walls,
stretching out the legs at odd angles.
We quit and head for the house to eat.

In the afternoon we argue about parts:
if this or that is the gall bladder,
whether the kidneys can be eaten.
Arlo wants to save the head
for head cheese, which he has no idea
how to make, so we throw it away,
along with various other parts.

I think about the projects
Arlo and I started, about what
we took apart long ago—radios, car
exhaust systems, machine shed doors
and leaky grease drums
for a pontoon boat never launched.
Pieces lie broken and scattered,
and I want to tell Arlo
to put the heart back, put the lungs
back, put the carburetor, and the tubes
and gears back. Put your sister's pink
umbrella back, that we thought
would make a perfect parachute
for jumping off the barn.
Yet not all of Arlo's ideas
have been totally disastrous.
We'll have pork chops this winter,
though some of the art
and much of the hog have been lost.

CHILL FACTORS

I like to wear my corduroy cap
when fall turns cool, but the wind
blows through that hole in back
above the adjustable strap.
I get my wife to sew a piece
of cloth, that matches pretty well,
inside the cap to block the hole,
and the next day I go and help Arlo
mount the bean header
on the combine. Arlo says
the piece of cloth on my cap
looks a little silly. I say
I don't know why it should look silly,
it seems practical to me.
But Arlo says that some might think
I'm too cheap to buy a cap
without a hole, if that's what I want.
I squat and tighten up some bolts
on the combine. It had occurred
to me the patch might look odd.
Arlo says that Old Man Brunner
has a patch like that on his cap.
Then Arlo's eyes light up.
He tells me what I should have sewed
in the back of my cap so no one
would even know it is a patch—
some fake fur the color of my hair,
or maybe, when my bald spot grows,
a piece of flesh-colored cloth.

Arlo says he can get me some cloth
to match my skin—his mother-in-law,
who's at the nursing home, has a pair
of stockings about the right shade.
Looking down at the Crescent wrench
in my hand, I consider how long
it would take to club Arlo senseless.
I drive home at noon and park
the pickup by the machine shed.
I take my cap off, study it,
put it on again, and look into
the rearview mirror, turning
my head from side to side.
I sit there wondering how long
it will take me
to open the door and get out.

THE ONLY PICTURE OF ARLO AND ME ALONE

The day was foggy. I forget why Arlo
was there—maybe to borrow a tool.
We stood in my muddy yard
a little apart, leaning back against
his Chevy pickup, and didn't even know
my wife, Janet, had sneaked
out on the porch with her camera.

Our wives can't get over how much alike
we look in the picture—Charlene says
maybe we are twins, separated at birth.
Arlo laughs and says he'd kill himself
if he found out I was his twin, and I say
I'd rather have a hog for a brother.

But we do resemble each other,
wearing identical seed corn caps,
hands deep in our pockets, and denim coats
open to the warming season.
And it's more than the clothes:
our faces have the same hard look
that matches the rocky land
in the background.
Maybe, like dogs and owners,
neighbors start to look alike.

We don't seem to be talking in the picture,
but brothers wouldn't need to say much.
I suppose we've just spit
and are about to shift
our overshoes in the mud, speculating
how soon a fellow might get into the field.

ARLO HEADS FOR KANSAS

Janet and I are in Arlo's yard
on Saturday morning, helping him
and Charlene put some last things
into their overloaded Ford.
The women take a long time
hugging and saying goodbye.
Arlo gets into the car, we sort of
shake hands through the window,
and we say not quite together,
"Well, take her easy."
It's cloudy and wet, too cold
for late June, a miserable day.

When Arlo hits the dip
at the end of the driveway,
a hole that he always talked about
filling in one of these days,
the low-riding Ford bottoms out
and blows a tire.

Arlo and I spent our younger days
driving on bad tires.
We changed many flats together
and now we fall into an old routine
we once executed with athletic precision.
He loosens the nuts. I set the jack
and get the spare. He jacks up
the car. I take off the flat

and put it in the trunk. He slides
the spare on and tightens nuts,
while I jack the car down.
He snaps the hubcap in place.
Then, smiling, we shake hands,
like a baseball pitcher and catcher
after a game-winning strikeout,
and put our left hands on each other's
shoulders in kind of a hug.

I tell him he better stop in town
and get that flat fixed.
"Yeah," he says, but I know he'll drive
straight through to Kansas,
figuring the odds are against
having two flats on the same day.
"Take her easy," I say. "Yup," he says,
"you too." In five seconds, the car
goes over a hill and out of sight.

PART IV ❀ THE STOOPED AND GRAY BOY

MY FIRST MORNING MILKING

I walk to the barn before a sign
of morning. The stars are sparks
in a black sky. Yellow light
from a window is on the blue snow.

Then my father and I
carry the milk pails to the house.
We bend over the sink, our heads
close together, and scoop up water
with our hands to wash our faces.

I smell bacon. The others come
downstairs, rubbing sleepy eyes.
I want to tell them what I know,
the mystery that goes away
when everyone wakes up and the sun
is a cold fire in the east window.

BLACKSMITH SHOP, JOHN FENNER & SON

The doorway, once just wide enough
for a lumber wagon, was made wider years ago
for a combine or corn picker. I step out of the sun
into cool shadows and the scent of burnt iron.
I give the old man my broken cultivator brace.
His scarred hands fit the fractured part together.
"Could be tricky," he says, "I'll get the boy."

The "boy," nearly seventy years old himself,
comes from the back of the shop and takes
the pieces. His arc welder spits dazzling light
that flashes up into corners above the rafters.
I loiter about, looking over tongs, hammers,
and obsolete wrenches hung on blackened walls.

The boy, stooped and gray, his welding mask
flipped up, comes forward and pauses, showing
the neatly welded piece and a trace of a smile
to the old man's trace of a nod.

BUYING THE COLD

Five below zero, old Orville
should have postponed his sale,
but a good bunch of us stand
in his yard, tapping the toes
of our five-buckle overshoes.
When Orville climbs
onto the tractor, and sits down,
we all feel the metal of the seat.
The auctioneer talks in puffs
of fog, "A Super-M, a Super-M,
best tractor ever made."
The auctioneer told him
to warm up the engine
beforehand, but Orville said,
"It'll start." He knows
how to jiggle the choke
exactly right—the machine
sputters, then roars,
and for a minute we are lost
in the thick clouds
billowing from the exhaust.
We move around the yard.
Our stiff denim coats
and bulky coveralls make
us look bigger than we are.
The ear-flaps on our caps
are down, and clear mucus
freezes in our grizzled beards.

The auctioneer goes on selling—
Arnold buys a shovel and pitchfork,
Wendell gets a steel wagon box.
I make the final bid
on a pile of straw bales
powdered with snow.
We still have faith enough
to buy into a few more winters.
After everything is sold
Old Man Brunner breaks
a three-foot brown icicle
from the roof of the calf shed
and asks, "What am I bid?"
We laugh, he tosses the ice spear,
and it shatters against the fence.

WINTER NEEDS

The morning after the blizzard
it's twenty below zero, but
the old man next door is out
sweeping snow off his car.
I put on boots and parka
and walk into a northwest wind.
He leans across the hood
and brushes clouds of snow
that powder my face
as I try talking to the back
of his old wool Mackinaw.
"You need some groceries, Louie?
I'll go and get them for you."
"I got enough groceries," he says.
Unbuttoning his coat,
he hunts through pockets for keys.
Ice creaks and splinters when
we force the frozen door.
His fingers shake, aiming the key
at the ignition slot.
"Are you going to visit your niece?
I'll take you. My car will be warm
in the garage and easy to start."
"No," he says. "I don't think I'll go
to Eunice's today.
Her kids get on my nerves."

He twists the key, the starter turns,
urr ... urr ... urr.
I offer something like a prayer
to fill the space between each "urr."
The miracle we both need comes
in sputters, rising to
a splendid roar as Louie gives
the motor lots of gas.
From under frosted brows
his burning eyes look up at me.
"See," he says, "it starts."
For two more minutes, he guns
the engine, then shuts it off.
"Aren't you going anywhere, Louie?"
"No," he says. "There's nowhere
I need to go today."

A REPORT ON MADNESS

We've been neighbors all our lives.
Yesterday I saw him
at the edge of the west forty,
with his rusty fishing rod,
casting into the cornfield.
When I got down there,
he was reeling in a daredevil lure
with corn leaves and bits of stalk
hanging on the hooks.
I asked him how they were biting.
It wasn't funny, I know,
but what else could I say?
A few more dry years
and any one of us might not be far
from fishing out of cornfields.
He kept casting.
His face was like one of those stones
he had picked for years from his field
and piled along the fence,
but the motion of his arm
made me think of a graceful dancer.
I stood back until he snagged
on a cocklebur and broke his line.
Then he let me
put my hands on his shoulders—
they felt warm and hard
through his denim coat—
and I turned him toward home.

THE COMING THAW

I can't believe you're not alive,
Christine. I thought we'd get through
one more winter at least,
with my old coat blocking drafts
under the kitchen door and plenty
of cobs to burn in the cookstove.
I know that over the last few years
bickering became a habit for us,
and now the farm, I hate to say,
is more peaceful with you gone.
But this blustery March afternoon
makes me want spring to come,
and as I clean the stove and carry out
the ashes, I'm thinking that
it's you I'd like to see walking up
from your garden in early summer,
bringing a handful of new onions
with the warm earth still on them.

FINDING THE WIND

The threshing machine had to be
lined up with the wind.
Even a breeze that didn't stir
cottonwood leaves could carry chaff
back into the grain wagon
and over the men pitching bundles.
To find the wind's direction,
my father picked up chaff or dust
and let it trail from his hand.
Standing beside him, I imitated
what he did, letting the light stuff go
gently from my fingers—it worked
every time. Now, I spend my days
fingering a computer keyboard,
but as I leave the house
on hot August mornings, I feel
the farmer left in me
needing to know how the wind blows,
and I pick up dry clippings of grass
from the yard and let them show me
a southern breeze
I didn't know was there.

A FARMER AS JANITOR

Last out of the locker room
after basketball practice,
exhausted, I sit down
in the empty bleachers
and watch Orville clean up.
His field is the gymnasium now.
He maneuvers a floor polisher
as if he were plowing,
making straight furrows,
turning after each round
in the headlands marked
by the base lines.

The spring in his step
surprises me. His face
looks bright and young
under the brim
of his green seed corn cap,
as if he might be thinking
about his next great crop
or remembering
the first time
he drove a tractor.

SOUNDS THAT CARRY

I rented out the land
for next year, picked the corn,
sold the cattle and machinery.
On one October day it's final.
The hell of it is I still feel
the familiar chill
of a clear fall morning
and smell the fine dryness
in the strong wind that blows
across the yellow grass and cornstalks.
Out of habit I head to the barn,
look into the empty stalls,
and hang up a brittle horse collar
that fell from a rusty spike.
I hear the neighbor's John Deere
start up, his cows bellowing,
and smaller sounds—even
the voices of kids in his yard—
that carry farther in the fall.

BREAKING EGGS

I'm disappointed, son,
in your imagination.
It's bad enough you broke
two dozen eggs, but you
just threw every one
of them on the ground
behind the chicken coop.
A solid, smooth surface
like a flat stone is best,
except it should
be vertical—a cement wall,
a silo, a tombstone would
be perfect, although
a live target might
be worth considering,
a cow, for instance.
Grasp the egg lightly
and wind up slowly,
using a high leg kick.
A smooth delivery is
essential, or the egg
could break in the release.
Throw from some distance,
but not too far—be close
enough to really see the splat.
The spanking still might not
be worth it, but at least
you'll know you've done it right.

PART V ❈ HEARING A MEADOWLARK

THE END OF THE DROUGHT

By midsummer, the corn leaves
had turned a dusty dark green
and curled into spikes—a field
of alien-looking plants that might
attack anyone who got too close.
This cold fall rain isn't enough
to wash that picture from my mind.
At breakfast, the toast is soggy,
and the cheddar tastes moldy.
We argue again. I need
every cent for hay this winter,
and she bought new wallpaper.

She wipes the table with a dishrag.
I stand up, go to the window, watch
the rain, then walk back to the table.
"The whole year has been a loss
all the way around. The rain
is way too late for this crop,
but I suppose we can't tell
what might happen if the subsoil
gets a good soaking," I say,
finding myself unrolling wallpaper.

RESTORING THE ECOLOGY

She raises flowers
and plants I couldn't even name.
The colors can be pretty
when they bloom—yellow,
red, orange, blue, purple.
But mostly the house
is overgrown with green:
pots full of slough grass,
some plants with waxy leaves,
trees with giant fan leaves
like elephant ears.
I complained that I needed
a machete, that any day
we'd hear the shrill caw
of some jungle bird.

One day I put a few drops
of herbicide
into the old coffee pot
she uses to water the plants.
I didn't really want to kill
them all, only to thin things out.
But the herbicide finished off
everything except a cactus,
which she didn't water.
The house had the desolate look
of a destroyed rain forest.
"Was it some disease?" she asked.
"Why did they all die like that?"

She was astonished
when I came home from town,
the pickup loaded down
with plants, and her delight
was something to see—
more plants than ever, some
she had never grown before.

Sometimes in the evening
when I sit reading my paper
and she's crocheting,
I look into the green around us
and imagine that a bird of paradise
is nesting somewhere back in there.

THE CONFESSIONS OF
A YOUNG FARM DOG

I sleep under the porch,
dreaming of leftover gravy.
In the morning when his foot
hits the boards above my head,
I come romping out, and though
he never seems to notice
my wagging tail, I'm always
enthusiastic, walking with him
as he does his chores.
I follow the tractor, even
when he goes fast and far
and I fall behind, or when
he plows or cultivates
back and forth over the field
a hundred times.
I am a little bothered
that he has never named me.
I would even settle for Shep
or Rover, but what the hell,
I have accepted the terms:
I help chase cattle,
and I bark when strange cars
drive into the yard.
For so little effort, I get fed
and occasionally patted
on the head—it's enough.

I'm happy that I'm no trouble
to him. When I'm old
he may need to put me
out of my misery.
I wouldn't want him feeling
too bad about such a thing,
but it might not come to that—
I've discovered the joy
of chasing cars and may end up
with my head under a tire.
Still, I could live a long life—
ten, twelve years—and die
in my sleep, dreaming
of a cute collie named Jennifer.
Sometimes my happiness
seems almost boundless.

COUNTRY CHURCH TECHNOLOGY

Now is the seventh Sunday of
the new PA system, and the words
of the sermon explode, echoing
like gunshots through a gulch.
Occasionally we can make out,
"God," "Jesus," "Hell," and "Give."
Old Man Brunner, who hasn't slept
through a sermon since they hung
those speakers on the walls,
sits stony faced, with his arms
crossed, and after church, he says
the cows in Harley's pasture
across the road will stop giving milk.
He talks about how sweet
it used to be, on a spring morning
when the windows were open, to hear
the song of a meadowlark in church.

FARM WORK

"A horse that farts will never tire.
  A man who farts is the man to hire."
                    —Unknown

1

I seemed lazy to myself.
Often I would stay in bed awhile
after my father called for chores.
On some days the chickens
went short on feed and water.

2

At threshing time, leather harness
creaked on the muscled shoulders
of the horses, and blocky men
in overalls pitched bundles of oats
into hayracks, building tall loads,
competing, joking, "You call that
a load? I could pee over that load."
Waiting in line at the threshing machine,
they squatted in the shade under the racks,
spitting snoose, farting, telling stories
they couldn't tell around the womenfolk,
but mostly talking about work.

3

I can look out of place in a suit and tie
with the best of them, but now,

applying for a job in a bank, I wonder
if the country lessons that once soaked
through my skin are totally worthless.
Something back there has to have value.
Does the manager behind the desk doubt
that I can be part of a hardworking team?
I feel the pressure in my gut build.

LEARNING THE CALL

As I walked away
from my grandfather's bed,
he called me back
and repeated his directions
for feeding the hogs:
take the rusty brown pail
that hangs beside the door
of the feed shed,
put five pails of ground feed
into the slop barrel,
and fill the barrel six inches
from the top with water.

He didn't instruct me
on calling the hogs,
but stepping into the pen,
I imitate his high-pitched,
nasal, one-of-a-kind call
that sounded like the word *pork*
half sung with an extra syllable:
"Poorerk, Poorerk, Poorerk."
But the call doesn't matter.
The hogs will come
if I yell, "Hey, you pigs,
come eat this slop."

After a week I no longer get
the formula exactly right.
I forget to hang the rusty pail
beside the feed shed door,
but the hogs go right on
with their slobbering, fighting
under the hot sun
for places at the troughs
in the sour-smelling hog yard.

Grandfather, you understood hogs
and must have known
it wouldn't matter to them
if you never came back.
But I'll get this batch fed out
for market according to your
directions. I'll work on my call.

DEER TICK NIGHTS

My wife and I are concerned
because we've seen deer come
to drink at the creek
in the grove behind the house.
We're safe from Lyme disease,
they say, if we remove ticks
within twelve hours.

The inspection routine pleases us:
every night we get naked
under the glaring overhead
bedroom light and come to know
each other's body better
than ever before—our lives
depend on it.

A CASSETTE OF TESTIMONIES COLLECTED IN A CHURCH BASEMENT AFTER A FUNERAL

"...the iron rule of lawns...may be stated as follows:
Short, green grass is the only normal, respectable thing
to have in your front yard."
—Sara Lowen, "The Tyranny of
the Lawn," *American Heritage*

1

What stands out in my mind about Neal
is how well he took care of his lawn.
His wife must have been proud
to have such fine looking grass.

2

I remember Neal was a hard worker
and never stayed long at the bar
drinking beer. He usually went home
most evenings and worked in his yard.

3

His grass was always carpet perfect.
I always wondered how
he got it so green. I guess he knew
what kind of fertilizer to buy.

4

Neal had a mechanical knack
and was always ready to help
if you needed to know about
a leaf blower or lawn mower.

5

No question, this was a man
who must have cared about nature.
When he visited us, he was always
looking at the grass and shrubs.

6

Neal saw the good in everything,
except winter, but he looked forward
to spring—before all the snow
was gone, he would be out with his rake.

7

He was a calm man.
The only time I ever saw him mad
was when the town council
put on that watering ban.

8

Neal seldom criticized anyone
but wasn't afraid to point out problems.
Once he wrote a letter to the pastor
about dandelions in the cemetery.

9

He was very considerate and careful.
When he used herbicide, he put string
on stakes around his yard with signs
warning people to stay off his grass.

10

Two things are so true about Neal
you could carve them on his tombstone:
he always looked cheerful
and kept a hell of a nice lawn.

WAKING

I fell asleep angry,
my fist doubled
under my leg.
How wonderful
it feels to wake
deep in the night
and open my hand
to moonlight so bright
I can count my fingers.

The Stones Take The Field

PART I ❀ SOFTLY LAUNCHED BY A BRIGHT
EXPLOSION

THE SECOND TRADE OF
THE STONE=BLOWER

The man they called
the stone-blower
winked at me as he opened
the trunk of his car
and brought out
dynamite sticks
and shiny brass caps.
We drove to the stubble field
in my father's pickup.
While the stone-blower dug
and planted his charges
under a rock, my father drove
the pickup to a safe distance.
I watched through the windshield.
The explosion sent black dirt
and rock pieces high into the air.
By late afternoon, I huddled
on the pickup floor and covered
my ears—the loud blast
and the blackness
of the explosions
had become too horrible.

But the stone-blower
also fixed beds.
He took my parents'
old cotton-padded mattress
and made it like new,

with inner springs.
Later, jumping on their bed,
I imagined myself a stone,
softly launched
by a bright explosion,
floating above danger,
thinking what a fine job
the stone-blower had done.

RETURNING WITH SNAKES

There was water
standing in the ditches
when I walked from school
and cut across
an alfalfa field,
which suddenly moved
with garter snakes,
dozens of them
on every side,
all heading the same
direction I was,
and though I felt
a fear tightening
around my throat,
the thrill pleased me,
and I was thankful
the snakes let me walk
with them, that while
we traveled together
their black and yellow
striped bodies,
moving in waves,
made me feel
I wasn't even walking
but floating like a raft,
and a tide of snakes
was sailing me home.

POUNDING THE MATTRESS

At breakfast
on the finest spring morning,
the day after school was out,
I heard meadowlarks singing
and thought I had nothing to do.
Then my mother and father
were carrying the mattresses
out into the yard
and laying them across rolls
of woven fence wire.
My father took the carpet beater,
like a giant tennis racket,
and made a couple of whacks
to demonstrate, and Mother said
it would be so much fun,
knocking the dust
and winter staleness
out of a mattress, but I soon learned
I'd rather be hitting a baseball
or fishing, and cursed my luck
as I pounded the place
where my parents slept.

BOYS AGAINST GIRLS

In our country school
we usually chose up sides
for softball games and seldom
played "boys against girls"
because it caused arguments.
But that year the girls
were sure they could win.
They outnumbered us,
and my two older sisters
could hit like Ted Williams.
Before noon on the day of the game
my face broke out with measles.
Everyone else had them before,
and there was no phone
to call parents, so the teacher
let me stay in school.
I felt fine, but she
made me stay inside
during the noon hour.

Alone in the silent room,
at the windows, I watched
my comrades getting trounced.
I walked to the mirror
above the wash basin
and swore at my red-speckled face.
Pictures of famous people

hung on the walls, and their eyes
looked down on me, followed me
wherever I moved in the room,
Washington and Lincoln
mocking my failure,
Florence Nightingale and Clara Barton,
smirking behind
their comforting nurses' faces.
I felt the shame of my spots
and tried to believe
I could make a difference
on the battlefield outside.

THE WALK

Behind the barn at Charley's place,
my cousins and I wonder how
the western movie hero
can jump from a balcony and land
astride his horse. Charley climbs
up on the roof of the barn's lean-to
while we make a horse
out of two bales of fresh hay.
Charley paces back and forth,
looking down at an eight-foot drop.
The danger fascinates us all.
He jumps, his knees apart and forward,
halfway into a sitting position,
and lands, straddling the bales.
"It works," he says,
"if you don't land wrong."

I take my turn, amazed and happy
I can actually do this stunt.
We make three more hay-bale horses,
and all four of us leap together,
launching ourselves out, sailing
lightly through the sweet alfalfa scent
in the air, landing like a posse
ready for hot pursuit.

Uncle Lawrence comes around the barn
and watches, shaking head. "If you guys
aren't careful," he says, "by tomorrow,
your voices will be six notes higher."

The next morning, there's some soreness
between my legs. I try singing
a few notes, noticing a crack in my voice,
but not enough to make me worry.
A quarter of a mile from school,
Sherill Ann meets me at the end
of her driveway, and we walk together.
"Why are you walking that way?" she says.
"What way?" I say. "It's how I walk."
By this time, the soreness is gone,
but I keep on walking with my legs
a little apart, liking that stride,
believing I'm ready for anything.

THE HEROIC AGE

The thermometer outside the kitchen window
says twenty-two below zero.
The car and pickup will not start.
As I put on extra clothes
for the almost three-mile walk to school,
I try to ignore my mother's concern.
"I think you better stay home," she says.

I've read about antarctic explorers:
Captain Scott and his companions,
in 1912, returning from the South Pole,
freezing to death ten miles from
their next food depot; Amundsen,
better prepared, winning the race
to the pole and returning safely.

"If you're going," my father says,
"don't take any shortcuts
across fields—stop at Peterson's
and warm up if you're cold."

There are only small patches of snow
in the ditches. The black, plowed fields
look hard as iron. As the gravel crunches
under my overshoes and frost gathers
on the brim of my cap, I imagine
a triumphant arrival at school,
the teacher and my schoolmates
admiring my brave journey.

I pass by Sherill Ann's place.
Almost lost in smoke, her father's Buick
stands in front of the house,
the motor running, warming up
so that Sherill Ann can ride in comfort.

I hurry on, but a hundred yards
from school Sherill Ann's father
pulls up beside me. I look
longingly at the short distance
to the finish, but I can't turn down
the ride without looking like a fool
so I get into the warm car.
"We saw you go by," he says.
"Why the hell didn't you come in?"
Sherill Ann laughs and says,
"Maybe his brain is frozen up.
He looks like a funny old man
with all that frost on his cap."

In the cloak room,
I take off layers of clothes,
trying to tell everyone I walked
practically the whole way,
but no one seems interested.
The teacher rings the bell,
and, still numb from the cold,
I sit down to a frozen, ordinary day.

THE ONE WHO DIED IN THE WAR

I was only seven,
and he was one of the older boys
who went to the country school
three miles west of ours.
I can't remember his face,
but once at a Sunday softball game,
he crawled on the grass
with me riding on his back.
Playing the horse to perfection,
he snorted, tossed his long hair,
and reared up, pawing the air,
the bend in his wrist
exactly horse-like
in a performance all for me.
Playing the rider but not too well
because I was laughing,
I gripped his T-shirt collar
and, waving a stick for a sword,
shouted, "Charge…charge!"

THE EVENING WE STOPPED PLAYING

On that still evening, we ran
on the soft grass, our laughing
voices echoing off the barn, until
one of us shouted, "Statues!"

and we stopped and held our poses.
Other voices carried all the way
from our neighbors' farm—we heard
his shouting voice, "You're not going!"

We heard her angry voice, too,
"I'm going, and you can't stop me."
We didn't even dare move, afraid
he'd somehow discover us listening

to his terrible voice, "Just get
it through your head you're not going!"
We felt shame, as if we weren't
supposed to hear her crying voice,

"I'm going, nothing can stop me!"
The car started and drove away.
We tried to run and laugh again
but the game wouldn't work—

no one could stand statue-like for long,
but when the others went into the house,
I stayed out by myself and was still,
stiller than the evening all around me.

BRUNNERSAURUS

Old Man Brunner, with his rough face,
shaggy eyebrows, and hooked nose,
looks like a troll.
He's gruff with children
and says we're spoiled and lazy,
but I can't help hanging around him.
Tonight at Wendell's place,
while the men play cards,
I sit on the floor and page through
the school book I brought along.
Old Man Brunner leans over
and asks what kind of nonsense
they're teaching kids these days.
I show him the pictures of dinosaurs,
explaining that they vanished
millions of years ago.
But Old Man Brunner snorts
and says animals like that
are still around, living in the mud
at the bottom of sloughs.
He says they come out
when a slough dries up
to look for a new home,
moving at night like a river
over fields and across country roads—
he knows of cars
that slid into the ditch
on their slimy bodies.

Riding home later,
alone in the back seat,
I look ahead at the gravel road,
trying to imagine what huge mysteries
might be out in the dark fields,
hoping, as the car goes over each hill,
the headlights will shine
on a herd of ancient dragons.
I fall asleep and dream of beasts
by the hundreds, each one
looking like Old Man Brunner,
crawling across the road,
and I wake up knowing
he will never be extinct.

THE SOPHOMORE BOYS AT SAINT MARY'S
GET A POETRY LESSON

Sister Charlotte read a poem she thought
teenaged boys would like, one about cars
racing through hills and valleys.
Benny made a car horn noise,
and then we all began
adorning each line with sound effects,
engines revving, screeching tires.
Sister Charlotte must have known
we were making fun of her,
but because of our
participation, she wanted to think
we actually enjoyed her reading of the poem,
and, I suppose, in a way, we did.

When Sister Charlotte read
the poems about love, we whispered
crude jokes, but we wondered
how she felt reading
"O, my love is like a red red rose...."
We knew this wasn't about Jesus.
As she spoke some lines by Shakespeare
she seemed to breathe a little faster
and her eyes became bright:
"In delay there lies no plenty;

Then come kiss me, sweet and twenty...."
In the lunch room later, Benny said
she must have been a hot one
before she became a nun.

That night, three of us drove the streets
in the warm September darkness
searching in vain for girls to pick up.
The soft wind brought the smell
of ripe cornfields right into town.
When we saw her by the church,
Benny said, "Should we pick her up?"
But no one laughed.
She was walking, I thought,
in beauty like the night.

THE STONES TAKE THE FIELD

When I was thirteen,
the cemetery had graves
only at the far end,
and we played baseball
on the vacant ground,
wary of bumblebees
visiting the wildflowers
in the deep, coarse grass.
With the tombstones
of prairie homesteaders
behind me, I flexed
my knees and pounded my glove.
Arlo, batting near the gate,
where my mother and father
are buried now, lifted
a fly ball into the sun.
I faded back, squinting at
the dizzy sky, measuring the arc.
On a dead run, I made the catch
above my right shoulder
and hopped, laughing, over
a headstone, confident
that nothing could trip me up.

PART II ❀ THE SWIRL OF AN ARC

MIDWAY IN NEEDS

I'm driving in South Dakota
and need to take a leak,
but the next town is too far.
The corn is not tall enough.
Here's a bridge I could go under,
but there might be mud
or quicksand or even snakes.
The trunk of that cottonwood tree
is too narrow to hide behind.
I could stand openly on the shoulder
of the road, but a car
might come along in midstream.
Feeling an intense need to release,
I scan the flat landscape.
Nothing is quite right.
Finally, I stop the car and walk
across a pasture toward the grove
of an abandoned farm place.
I follow a path through the trees,
coming out in a sunlit yard.
And there, loading straw bales
onto a Ford pickup, is a strong,
beautiful woman, wearing
tight jeans and a red flannel shirt.
I stop, shifting my weight
from one foot to the other.
How will I explain myself?

AFTERNOON IN JANUARY

I'm in the cattle yard,
shoveling snow from a feedbunk,
beginning to believe
this long winter will never end
and I'll spend the rest of my life
alone in the cold,
making sure that animals are fed,
when I hear a strange honking
from high overhead—geese,
strung out in "V" formations
across the cold gray sky,
heading south.
Why are they so late?
Always a hard, responsible worker,
I wonder, almost with a sneer,
at their incompetence.
Maybe each goose in this flock
is from another flock, the one goose
who's never ready to go,
and all these stragglers,
by some miracle, found one another.
They seem determined enough.
Their squawks sound happier
than any I've ever heard in the fall.
And suddenly I'm happy watching them.
It doesn't matter
that when they finally arrive south
it will be time to come back.
Now, they're on their way.

AFTER HEAVY SPRING RAINS

I'm afraid I planted the corn too late.
At the lake, I leave my fishing gear
in the car and sit under a tree,
thinking all day, adding up my losses.
In the late afternoon, a boy
walks up from the shore,
carrying a homemade willow pole
and a handsome string of bluegills.
His jeans are neatly patched,
and he's wearing big shoes
that once were someone else's.
If I offer him ten dollars
for that string of fish,
I'd have something to show for the day,
and he'd have a lot of money, for a boy.
But then he wouldn't have the fish
to show his father, who this minute
might be coming home
from the field. And his mother—
maybe it happens she's been wondering
what to make for supper, and he
could hand her these beautiful fish.

As he comes closer, the low sun
glitters through the fish, whose scales
look like blue jewels and flecks of gold,
a treasure I can barely resist,

but I only say,
"That's a pretty bunch of fish,"
and his smile, a provider's smile,
which I'll carry home somehow,
is my catch of the day.

AT BREAKFAST

"That's the last of the coffee," she said,
  pouring a few drops into his cup.
"It's time you went out to work anyway."

"I don't know if I'll plow today," he said.
"Look, the sky is clouding up.
  It might start to rain."

"The sun is shining," she said.
"I need to wash the dishes so I can go
  to the beauty shop in town."

"The tractor engine," he said,
"made strange noises yesterday
  and might explode if I try to start it."

"If I don't get to town early," she said,
"I'll never have time to get a perm
  and do all the grocery shopping."

"Giant, man-eating lizards," he said,
"have crawled up out of the slough
  and are roaming around in the north forty."

"We both have work to do," she said.
"You've taken twice your usual time
  eating breakfast today."

"I see white on the horizon," he said.
"Maybe a glacier is moving over the field.
 There's no sense in taking chances."

"Oh, all right," she said.
"You can come along.
 I suppose we can eat in town."

NIGHT RITUAL

At ten o'clock he switches on
the television set to watch
the weather report.
This morning when he walked
in the wet grass, his senses confirmed
the forecast of the night before:
scattered thunderstorms before dawn,
clearing morning skies, southwest winds
at five miles per hour, high of seventy-five.
But he had not known he would find
in the pasture his best cow dead
from a lightning strike.
Now, as he watches the forecast,
distraction clouds the ritual.
He remembers when he was young,
half drunk outside a dance hall,
throwing a beer bottle high off
into the dark above the parking lot,
thrilled by the danger,
not knowing where it would strike,
and he wonders how to warn his son
against such recklessness.
And his daughter—he can't even
imagine a way to tell her about
that boy, the one with the haircut.
The screen maps a few days
of the future in numbers
and colored lines and arrows.

Fearing unpredicted storms,
he wonders when the next front
will pass over his head.

MAN STRANDED OVERNIGHT
IN BARN DURING BLIZZARD

We hadn't been married long.
She was new to farm life and said
it wouldn't be so bad if only
on Sunday there were no chores.

The barn was almost dark inside,
and when I lit the kerosene
lantern I knew that she
was lighting the lamps in the house.

All of a sudden the snow swept hard
against the north wall when the wind
changed, making a soft moan.
I wondered if she heard it too,

as she put supper on the stove.
By this time she couldn't see
the barn from the window
above the kitchen table.

I fed the calves most of the milk,
gave the cats a feast, and with
one pail, stepped out into
a swirl of gray and darkness.

I knew at once I could miss our house
and be lost, and, cursing the storm
that left no choice, I felt my way
along the wall back to the barn door.

I was safe enough—a barn
well built with the loft full of hay
would hold in the heat from
the cattle. I'd never freeze,

but she wouldn't know if I
started for the house and got lost
in the storm. With supper getting cold,
she could only worry and wait.

I have no hero's story.
I put down straw and tried
to sleep between two cows until
the wind let up near dawn,

when I left the barn, able to see
the lamplight in the kitchen window
through the drifting snow.
On the couch but not asleep,

she heard me at the door,
and was beside me, helping
with my coat, both of us talking
at once about our night apart.

I felt as though I should apologize
for the storm as she warmed
the coffee and leftover supper.
At six in the morning we sat

at the table, having talked away
every fear except the one I had
of saying it would soon be time
to go out and milk the cows again.

THE JOYS OF SPRING

When I've been hauling out manure
all afternoon from the cow yard,
and the highway, from the end
of my lane to the field,
is covered thickly with manure
that fell from the spreader,

when I'm spreading the last load
and see a black Cadillac approach
the coated stretch of road
and slow way down (its driver
probably wishing his luxurious car
had the option of flight),

and when I see the splatter
cover his wheels and fenders
with a barnyard smell he'll carry
into the city, his car stinking for weeks
from manure baked on his muffler
and catalytic converter,

then I breathe deeply the spring air
and think how good life is on earth.

REINVENTING THE REUNION

At noon the tractor sits idling
on the gravel road, while I stand
beside the mailbox, reading a letter
from the class reunion organizers.
I don't mind being a farmer,
but I'd like to go as something else.
I picture myself wearing
a casual linen suit and Italian shoes.
Would it be possible
to rent a Jaguar for a day?
Could my wife—with a trip
to the beauty shop,
the right clothes, some practice
with a French accent—pose as my lover?
(Floyd, Ruthann, let me introduce
my friend, Angelique.)

Driving the tractor
up the driveway, I'm cruising
in the red Jaguar convertible
on county roads, back through miles
of summer and green cornfields,
Angelique's golden hair
flying in the wind.

Nonchalantly, I tell old classmates
I'm working on a script for a movie

in which Angelique will star.
Since the film will be set
in Minnesota, Angelique and I
are living there just to get
an authentic feel for the place,
but come fall we'll head for Paris.
And those who once cruised
Main Street in their hot cars,
who now have settled
for practical family vans,
eye the Jaguar enviously—someone
asks what kind of mileage I get.
Hanging my sunglasses on my pocket,
I look at Angelique and say, "A lot."

LIVING ALONE

It happens like this: walking on a windy street,
you hear a sweet voice call your name.
You look around but see only strangers.
Later, that night, the phone stops ringing
before you pick it up. In the morning,
you see tracks in the fresh snow—someone
walked up your driveway and, five steps
from your door, turned back to the road.
Maybe a mysterious, beautiful woman,
wearing white fur boots, approached
your house in the dark. Where she turned back
her wine-red velvet skirt swirled an arc
in the snow—at least she came that far.
Hunching your shoulders in the cold, you look
for a long time at the delicate footprints
and think about leaving your porch light on.

PART III ❋ PAST FULL BLOOM

FOUR KINDS OF LILACS

"Why don't you turn at the next corner,"
she said, "and take another road home.
Let's go past that farm with all
the different colored lilacs."

"That's seven miles out of the way,"
he said. "I wanted to plant the rest
of the corn before evening. We
can look at lilacs some other time."

"It'll take only a few minutes"
she said. "You know that lilacs
aren't in bloom for long—if we
don't go now, it will be too late."

"We drove past there last year,"
he said. "They're like any other lilacs
except for the different colors. The rest
of the year, they're all just bushes."

"They're lilac, purple, white, and pink,"
she said. "And today, with no breeze,
the scent will hang in the air—no flowers
smell as good as lilacs in the spring."

"I thought of planting lilacs once,"
he said, "for a windbreak in the grove.
The good smell lasts only a few days.
I suppose we can go, if we hurry."

"Now slow up," she said.
"Last year, you drove by so fast
   we couldn't even get a good look.
   It wouldn't hurt to take it easy."

"Well, there they are," he said,
"and looking pretty scraggly—past
   full bloom already. You should
   have thought of doing this sooner."

A RETIRED FARMER WORKING
AS A GREETER AT WAL=MART

The store went up last year outside of town.
There was a cornfield where I'm standing now,
smiling, saying hello, and handing out ads
for plastic purses, towels, and microwaves.
The job doesn't pay much, but neither did farming.
Pete, my old neighbor, wearing clean overalls,
comes in. I say, "Hey, you lazy fart, I see
you're taking a day off to loaf in town."
And Pete says, "You should talk, getting paid
for standing around in an air-conditioned store."
While we talk about the rain last night,
the possibility of early frost, the price of hogs,
a dozen customers pass by ungreeted,
and I feel uneasy about not doing my job.

In one way, it's like farming—spending hours
on the tractor, with lots of time to daydream.
Now, I invent secrets I'd like to tell customers.
"Every third mineral water bottle is filled
with Russian vodka. Snakes have been found
in the cups of the imported brassieres."
But I only say, "Hello, how are you,"
and send them on their way down the aisles,
which are nothing like rows of corn.

A FATHER AND SON STANDING
AT THE RUINS

My old man never wanted much.
He wouldn't ask me to take him anywhere.
His motto was, "Don't go to any trouble for me."
The Sunday drive was my idea,
but I began to think I'd made a mistake
bringing him to the farm where he was born.
Scanning the yard, he said,
"Not much left worth looking at."
We found a padlock on the door
of the farmhouse. Trying to see inside,
I parted the six-foot sunflowers
and cupped my hands around my eyes,
peering through a dark window.
"Can you see anything?" he said.
I made space for him, and we stood
a long time, looking into an empty room.
"I remember that crack," he said,
"down there in the baseboard."

Back in town, when I took his hand
and helped him stand up from the car,
he laughed—as if we were partners
in a joke. "Well," he said,
"we went a long way to see a crack."

AFTER WATCHING A TV WILDLIFE SPECIAL, OLD MAN BRUNNER DREAMS HE'S A PENGUIN

He's driving his battered Dodge truck
across a white plain, thinking he's lost
in a Dakota blizzard, when
he sees penguins walking up ahead.
The truck stalls, he steps out,
and follows them over the snow.
The sleeves of his chore coat
turn into black flippers, and white feathers
sprout from his chest—he's one of them,
an emperor penguin in the Antarctic,
headed for Cape Crozier, sixty miles away.

Old Man Brunner has no idea how
he will choose a mate—the female penguins
all look about the same.
Then he sees one, perched high on a rock,
who reminds him of Mae West,
his favorite movie star, the full,
soft body (he has had enough leanness
in farming the dusty prairie), the way
she cocks her head, flirting so openly.
Her fluttering penguin eyelashes say,
"Come up and see me."
He puts his right flipper around her waist,
holds her close, her warm breast ballooning
against his, and they waltz across the ice
and lie down under a warm snow blanket.

Afterwards, Old Man Brunner feels young again.
The swaggering penguin walk
is natural to him, as he leaves to feed
with the males, who playfully
bump shoulders with one another
and congratulate him: "Still can get
the engine cranked up, you old son of a gun."

But on the journey back, he aches with fear.
The males will take over incubating
the eggs while the females go and eat.
Old Man Brunner has always thought
birds stupid, but at least with pheasants,
or even chickens, the roosters
have sense enough to leave hatching
and caring for the young to the womenfolk.

Old Man Brunner doesn't want the egg.
But an old force, like obsolete,
rusty farm machinery moving inside him,
makes his head bob, signaling
Mae West he's ready to accept.

He stares down in disbelief at the egg
balanced on his feet, which still
look like his cracked work shoes.
He sighs and squats. Huddled among the males
at the end of the earth, in howling gales
and darkness, Old Man Brunner
feels as though the egg is the world
cracking under him.

Hungry, faint, the warmth flowing down
from his body, he sees her on the horizon
in the winter dawn stillness,
Mae West coming home, and he has,
right here on top of his feet,
this new life she hasn't yet seen.

Already in the world between
sleep and waking, Old Man Brunner realizes
this dream is the best story he knows,
but it's one he won't be telling
to the boys at Elmer's Bar.

THEY BUY A PAIR OF PANTS AT PENNY'S

"Here's a nice navy blue pair," she said.

"My brown pair is all right, and I've
still got the gray pair," he said.

"The seat is almost worn through
on the brown pair, and you
have never had a blue pair," she said.

"I don't like blue. Blue shows the dirt
and everything else," he said.

"Here's a size forty," she said.

"A forty is too big. The gray pair
is thirty-eight," he said.

"The gray pair looks too tight on you.
We can always bring this one back,
or I can take it in if it's too big.
You should get a light blue shirt
to go with it," she said.

"I've got enough shirts," he said.

HIS ELDERLY FATHER AS A YOUNG MAN

This happened before I met your mother:
I took Jennie Johanson to a summer dance,
and she sent me a letter, a love letter,
I guess, even if the word *love* wasn't in it.
She wrote that she had a good time
and didn't want the night to end.
At home, she lay down on her bed
but stayed awake, listening to the songs
of morning birds outside her window.
I read that letter a hundred times
and kept it in a cigar box
with useless things I had saved:
a pocket knife with an imitation pearl handle
and a broken blade,
a harmonica I never learned to play,
one cuff link, an empty rifle shell.

When your mother and I got married,
I threw the letter away—
if I had kept it, she might wonder.
But I wanted to keep it
and even thought about hiding places,
maybe in the barn or the tool shed,
but what if it were ever found?
I knew of no way to explain why
I would keep such a letter, much less
why I would take the trouble to hide it.

Jennie had gone to California
not long after that dance.
I pretty much got over
wanting to see her just once more,
but I wish I could have kept the letter,
even though I know it by heart.

CPR OR NO CPR

We bring Aunt Martha to the nursing home.
They weigh her, barely a hundred pounds,
and we help her lie down for a nap.
She closes her eyes, and the lines
of her frail body almost vanish
in her loose-fitting black dress.
I remember how this woman,
after her husband died,
ran the farm herself,
operating tractors and combines,
digging post holes and stretching barbed wire,
dehorning cattle and castrating pigs.
She cooked, too, and baked bread,
and fixed her daughters' hair.
Everyone knew Martha could do anything.
Now, the nurse adjusts the Venetian blinds
and, speaking softly, tells us
we'll have to talk it over with Martha
when she wakes up and decide which box
to check on her chart—"No CPR" means
that if she ever stops breathing,
they won't try to bring her back.
Standing near her bed, we talk in whispers,
wondering how we'll raise this subject,
when, without opening her eyes, she speaks
in the voice she once used to direct
a crew of men shelling corn or filling silo,
"I'll kill anyone who brings me back."

NEAR THE END OF THE MILLENNIUM

Along the old fence line
between my neighbor's field
and mine, I bored a new
post hole, discovering on
this unplowed strip of ground
a topsoil layer so deep
it almost had no end.
Our fields were once that rich,
and it all disappeared
from right under our noses.
For awhile the fences saved
some of the wildness, too.
Around the posts and wire,
the tumbleweeds grew thick,
and there were chokecherry bushes
where pheasants could nest or hide.
But that was before herbicide,
before we ripped out
most fences to make our fields
so huge they're visible
from deep in outer space.

DAYS OF YESTERYEAR

The cornfields beyond the highway
by the Kmart parking lot remind me
that once all of this was tallgrass prairie.
In front of the store, three adolescent girls
climb onto the electric horse and ride,
laughing, bucking, three pairs of legs
in blue jeans rocking astride,
the machine playing calliope music,
the "William Tell Overture,"
brown, blonde, and black hair
flying in the October wind.
When the horse stops, they put in
another quarter, again and again.
Watching from my car window,
hearing that music,
I imagine my childhood hero,
the Lone Ranger, watching, too.
He's an old man now—the mask
can't conceal his age, though it covers
his gray temples and the wrinkles
around his eyes. He suddenly sees,
in the bouncing three on horseback,
the enormity of his sacrifice
to become a champion of justice.
And Tonto, showing his years,
behind the left shoulder
of the masked man, says,
"Kemo Sabe, you riding Silver
at a full gallop was a thrilling sight,
but this...but this...."

ACKNOWLEDGMENTS

Thanks to the following periodicals and anthologies in which many of these poems first appeared:

The Blue Skunk Companion, Blue Unicorn, Bottomless Pot of Coffee, Buffalo Bones, Colorado North Review, Commonweal, From Seedbed to Harvest (Seven Buffaloes Press), Great River Review, Hurākan, Lake Region Review, The Midwest Quarterly, Manna, Nebraska Territory, North Coast Review, North Country Anvil, North Dakota Quarterly, The North Stone Review, Plainsong, Poetry NOW, Preposterous (Orchard Books), Spoon River Quarterly, Tempest, Writers and Writing (Minnesota State University System), Zone 3.

Several poems in *Old Man Brunner Country* first appeared in the chapbook *Keeping Between the Fences* (Westerheim Press).

ABOUT THE AUTHOR

Leo Dangel was born in South Dakota in 1941 and grew up on a farm near Freeman and Turkey Ridge. He attended colleges in Minnesota and South Dakota and received an MA degree in English from Emporia State University in Kansas. He taught literature and writing for twenty-five years at Southwest State University in Marshall, Minnesota.

Twelve hundred copies of *Home From the Field* were printed during the great winter of 1997. The types are Monotype Dante and Adobe Poetica. Special thanks to Cheryl Jacobsen for creating the calligraphy on the front cover and to Kristin Pichaske for drawing the portrait of the author. Typographic design is by Shari DeGraw. The cover photograph, "Misty Mood," was taken by Lyle Wessale and is used by permission.